DIANNE WIEBE

GEORGE ALFRED TOWNSEND & GATHLAND

A Journalist and His Western Maryland Estate

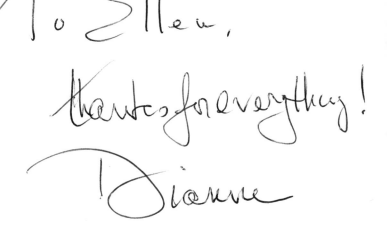

To Ellen,

thanks for everything!

Dianne

Charleston · London

THE
History
PRESS

Published by The History Press
Charleston, SC 29403
www.historypress.net

Copyright © 2014 by Dianne Wiebe
All rights reserved

Cover image: Antique postcard reproduction. *Courtesy of Gathland State Park Museum.*

All images, unless stated otherwise, are courtesy of
Gathland State Park Museum Archives.

First published 2014

Manufactured in the United States

ISBN 978.1.62619.471.7

Library of Congress CIP data applied for.

To GATH...You are not forgotten.

CONTENTS

FOREWORD

$\mathscr{I}$ was educated through my sophomore year of college in my home state of Maryland, a state where George Alfred Townsend (Gath) had many influences. However, Gath was unfortunately unknown to me and countless others educated in the same period. I was aware of the work of other great Maryland writers like Edgar Allan Poe and H.L. Mencken, so why not Gath? It wasn't until the Maryland Park Service promoted me to superintendent of the South Mountain Recreation Area that I finally discovered Gath.

In 1990, I found myself entrusted with the stewardship of Gath's former estate in Crampton's Gap on South Mountain. It is now called Gathland State Park. The lack of reference to Gath during the course of my education seemed wrong ,and I felt duty bound to somehow make it right. In 2009, Dianne Wiebe joined the staff at the museum at Gathland State Park. With her background in journalism, local history and museum management, she developed an immediate and lasting connection to Gath. Dianne conducted research, connected with some of Gath's descendants and collected stories from visitors and local residents, thereby establishing herself as the Gath subject matter expert that the park desperately needed. Her fascination with Gath's life and literary accomplishments prompted her to write this book. An author with a journalism background and several books to her credit, she decided that Gath, who loved the fame and recognition of his stellar career, had called on her to keep his legend alive and flourishing into the twenty-first century.

Through *George Alfred Townsend and Gathland: A Journalist and His Western Maryland Estate*, Dianne Wiebe reminds us that Gath, the youngest of all the correspondents covering the American Civil War, changed the face of journalism by pioneering syndication. Gath was embedded with the troops of Major General George B. McClellan during the 1862 Peninsula Campaign and investigated (and authored a book about) the *Life, Crimes, and Capture of John Wilkes Booth*. Gath was a witness to Booth's execution; dined with generals, senators and heads of state; and was photographed many times by Mathew Brady. He helped define the role of a war correspondent by placing himself in harm's way and producing accurate and timely descriptions for anxious readers. His craft is as relevant today as it was during the Civil War, placing Gath with the likes of Edward R. Murrow, Gloria Emerson, Walt Whitman, Ernest Hemingway, Ernie Pyle, Michael Herr, Marguerite Higgins, Joe Sacco and Daniel Pearl. Postwar, Gath succeeded as an editorialist, novelist, poet, playwright and architect. A journalist herself, Dianne Wiebe is uniquely qualified to interpret Gath's career and introduce his legacy to a generation of people who, like me, find reference to him absent in their formal educations. Dianne Wiebe, with this book, is beginning to right the wrong I first perceived as a young park superintendent.

Systems of public parks, whether local, state or national, have become the keepers of many of our great nation's historical and cultural treasures. Gathland State Park preserves more than one of these treasures. Remnants of old charcoal hearths are found at Gathland. The charcoal was used to fuel our nation's first industry forging cannons for the Revolution in great iron furnaces. During the Civil War, Gathland State Park was the scene of fierce fighting and action within Confederate general Robert E. Lee's Maryland Campaign. Northern victory in the Maryland Campaign gave President Lincoln the confidence to issue the Emancipation Proclamation. The action at Gathland State Park was therefore a catalyst for the beginning to the end of slavery in the United States. The Appalachian National Scenic Trail bisects Gathland State Park, so Gathland provides a respite for weary hikers along our nation's first National Scenic Trail. The trail is a ribbon of land stretching from Maine to Georgia, a footpath of over two thousand miles. Gath was so inspired by this ground that he established his estate there, making Gathland significant to the journalistic history of our nation. Dianne Wiebe understands the uniqueness of this special place, a quality she shares with Gath, and calls our attention to it. Through her excellent work, she has kept the legend of Gath alive and flourishing into the twenty-first century.

—Dan Spedden
Superintendent (retired), South Maryland Recreation Area

Acknowledgements

To Dan Spedden who always knows how to make good things happen. To Ellen Shourd, who bravely edited my first draft; Greg Bartles, who carefully scanned the photos I needed; and to Ross Kimmel, who dug those photos out of hiding. To Janice Teeter, my muse and life coach. To John Muller, Anne Long, Jackie McCullough and Susan Fair, all of whom encouraged me. To David Rasmussen, his sister Elizabeth Forster and especially to his mother, Dorothy Rasmussen, and to Dale Swope for their contributions to the project. To Patrick Hiatt, who filled in some mythological blanks. To John Frey and Elizabeth Howell at the Washington County Library. To Ruthanna Hindes and Jerry Shields, whose earlier books provided a factual basis for all that has been written since.

To the Gathland State Park Museum founders, who created an archive of photos and documents from various resources, including the Maryland Hall of Records, the University of Delaware and the Maryland Department of Natural Resources. Unless otherwise noted in the captions, all the photographs are courtesy of the Gathland State Park Museum archives.

And to all the visitors who visited the Gathland museum and urged me to tell the story in book form.

AUTHOR'S NOTES

*T*here are many and varied reasons why these small-market books get written and published, but almost all of them can be categorized as a labor of love. We are consumed by the desire to save a person or a legend or an event for posterity and to rescue an interesting story from obscurity.

I "met" George Alfred Townsend (GATH) when I started work at the museum in Gathland State Park in Western Maryland, on the site of his former estate and his monumental War Correspondents Memorial. I strongly suspect that I got the job not because I had been a journalist but because all the other applicants were more interested in interpreting the Civil War, a major attraction in this area.

In the archives, I discovered a man of many talents who was ambitious, charismatic, larger than life, classically educated and immensely energetic. I quickly fell into his thrall. A bit of P.T. Barnum and part H.L. Mencken, I was impressed by his success but distressed by the shabby condition of his legend. It was at that point that I became GATH's handmaiden.

The journey that is this book has been an amiable one. GATH has brought hundreds of interesting visitors to the museum and gave me entrée to the like-minded and congenial community of local history buffs. Descendants from both coasts have visited and contributed to his return to prominence and provided personal correspondence that grants us additional access to the man inside the public figure.

I learned a lot from GATH about legacy. Visitors to the museum who are parents of adult children immediately understand his disappointment on learning that what he was able to leave them—his parenting, his rather brilliant career and his fabulous estate—was, for whatever reason, not important to them. It is our children who create our legacy from what is of value to them. Where his children might have disappointed, I took up the cause.

Although two other writers have published books on GATH, I had the advantage of being able to bring him into the twenty-first century and help restore the prominence and recognition he feared would be lost. Documenting the one hundred years since his death allowed me to showcase his place in the continuum and the way in which people, places and events find their place in it.

With the telescopic lens of hindsight, it is possible to write the happy ending GATH was denied in life. Robbed of his health, energy and the reputation he hoped would allow him to join his colleagues in eternal literary glory, his creative talent once again serves him well.

Using his contacts, and what we now call "networking," his talent for design and a masterful gift for fundraising, he pulled off his most important achievement, the one that grants him his most abiding wish—that he will not be forgotten. With the Arch, he leaves an unmistakable calling card, with his trademark mythological references and quotes from antiquity, one that is ornate, heavily embellished and cleverly expresses all the characteristics and achievements that made him proud to be GATH.

He must have grown impatient, waiting all those years to be invited back, finally to receive the recognition he knew he deserved.

Introduction

*G*eorge Alfred Townsend (GATH) was a prolific and successful writer who for more than four decades reigned supreme among journalists in this country. He was energetic, determined and talented, though some accounts describe him as pompous, ostentatious and occasionally combative. He was definitely flamboyant and very much an artist in everything he attempted—and he attempted everything that caught his interest.

From a childhood of very modest circumstances, he rose to fame and fortune he might never have imagined possible, but with talent, hard work and perseverance, he managed to achieve an impressive career in journalism in the late nineteenth century. With his new wealth, he created a unique and beautiful estate in Western Maryland, tailored to his aesthetic and domestic needs.

Townsend wrote about everything in daily columns, letters, books, pamphlets, essays, lectures, addresses, plays and poems. His subject matter was boundless, from battles of the Civil War to the Mormon Trials to Uriah Levi's restoration of Jefferson's Monticello. He ventured into investigative journalism to cover Lincoln's assassination and the subsequent trial of the assassins. After his service as a correspondent for the *New York Herald* in the Civil War, he rose steadily in the field of journalism, and by 1870, he had appeared in newspapers all over the country.

Townsend came to Western Maryland already well known in the newspaper world, seeking a quiet and peaceful place to build a summer home. Here, he would write, entertain and raise his family in the manner of a country gentleman. Over a ten-year period, the summer home became an estate consisting of several very large and elaborate homes, outbuildings and gardens. He was a man of the world, but Gapland, his Boonsboro estate, was home for the last forty years of his life; it was the place he loved most, the haven he called home.

Late in life, good fortune abandoned him. His fame—and the wealth that came with it—evaporated, and he ended his life impoverished, forlorn and forgotten. Gapland, his lavish estate, and the Arch were the culmination of his dreams, symbols of his wealth and fame and a testament to his creative artistry.

The landscape today is not very different from the way it appeared in 1881, when Townsend first encountered it. Few traces of the Civil War battlefield it had once been remained at Crampton's Gap; it was ready to become the site of his country estate and, finally, the monument. One hundred years later, few traces of his luxurious estate remain at Gathland, now a state park, but his legacy is preserved.

Today, even the oldest residents of the area remember him only as a local legend from their childhood, when their families held picnics on the grounds of the vanishing estate, already deteriorated and overgrown with vegetation. But the monument he designed and built remains pristine, still a commanding presence and as startling to the visitor today as it was when it was completed in 1896. Rising suddenly before the travelers as they climb the hill on which it stands, it is a bold reminder of the creative genius of George Alfred Townsend, the man who became GATH. Famous in his own time, then forgotten, his legend is flourishing once again.

1

George Alfred Townsend,
the Beginning

*B*orn in 1841 to Stephen Townsend, a Methodist circuit-riding preacher, and his wife, Mary Milbourne, young George Alfred Townsend knew nothing of the luxury that defined his later years. The Townsend home had few books beyond the Bible, and his parents were able to provide only the barest necessities of food and clothing for their sons, George and his brothers, Stephen Emory and Ralph Milbourne. The frequent moves necessitated by his father's chosen profession also made it difficult to have friends or to be part of a community—a lonely life for a child.

From a distance of more than sixty years, writing his memoirs, he tells the story of his childhood. His was a strict upbringing. He describes his mother as "the Methodist of the family, six years my father's senior and of a rigid but impressive type, who persuaded him, an orphan out of his trade of carpenter and builder, to take up the Methodist ministry."

Apparently, his father lacked both the zealotry and the income to dedicate himself solely to the ministry and later studied medicine, becoming a physician at the age of forty-eight. For the last twenty-four years of his life, he was both preacher and physician, and by his seventieth birthday, the elder Townsend had earned a PhD. Still, money problems plagued him. Late in his life, letters to his son express his continuing concerns with financial dealings.

Townsend had two brothers and two other siblings who died in infancy. During his years in high school, his older brother, Steven Emory, was killed while fighting in Nicaragua with American forces. He was just twenty-one, and Townsend describes him as "a noble boy, generous, frank, brave, ambitious and intelligent," but wrote that "he has ever been a source of trouble and anxiety to my father." Still, Townsend proposed to write a memorial for Emory. A younger brother, Ralph Milbourne, became a physician and died at the age of thirty-two.

In his memoirs, Townsend complains of the life he was subjected to as a child: "My childhood was disagreeable, not to say squalid. We were properly educated and travelled without pay as preacher's sons, seldom had any money, sometimes were dressed secondhand, were debarred from all but 'moral' and therefore stupid amusements, and felt no piety, though surrounded by the sacerdotal life." Perhaps the impecunious situation in which he spent his boyhood influenced his later preference for lavish surroundings and a life of adventure and epicurean extravagance:

> *The ten years I recall as a preacher's son are uncongenial. I think of the Revivals with unconcern, where people were exhibiting public paroxysms under the fear of "Sin" and bawling, singing and frenzied prayer hardly ruffled the urchinhood banked upon the pulpit steps. Among the things I look back on with pain is the small care taken of the person politeness of the preacher's offspring. All week the preacher was studying; everybody's family had the call before his. The first thing that awakened me was novelty, books, newspapers. No paper but the* Christian Advocate *came to the family; we borrowed the highly interesting daily paper.*
>
> *When I was thirteen the Boston weekly came to the Pennsylvania hamlet by a peddler, and I read patriotic legends of the American Revolution. The theatre cited me first to see* Uncle Tom's Cabin. *That curtain unfolded a magic world. It is certain that I had literary precocity, for two small papers were issued in my childhood for both of which I wrote successfully. I won an honor at the High School for Composition on a public occasion.*

Though Townsend was born in Georgetown, Delaware, the family moved often, living in Snow Hill, Cambridge, Princess Ann and other communities on Maryland's Eastern Shore, as well Port Deposit, Chestertown and various towns in Delaware. In each location, good schools were found. At Chestertown, he attended a school offered by Washington College. Later, at the age of ten, he attended the Newark Academy, which later became the University of Delaware. Sometime between 1853 and 1855, the family moved to Philadelphia for what would become a more permanent home.

Whatever drawbacks his father's itinerant life presented for his sons, there were obvious advantages. Townsend was keenly observant, and much of what he learned in these various environments took hold in his mind, remaining there until the writer he would become had fully emerged. In his early adolescence, he was already writing for public consumption, sketching and painting as well and attending good schools. However grim his portrait of the past, at least by the time of his adolescence, he was getting a good education and starting to find the direction his life would take.

In 1856, Townsend began high school at Central High School of Philadelphia, an early public school still in existence, although at a different location. Then and now, the school grants advanced degrees to students who complete the required coursework, and Townsend was awarded a master of arts degree in 1860. He was just nineteen. A document found in possession of a descendant states that the master of arts degree was awarded on February 16, 1865, but no explanation is given for this, and there is no evidence that Townsend completed further schooling after 1860.

During his time at Central High School, he wrote articles for various local publications and was active with school publications. The school offered a rigorous education, and Townsend excelled at writing and presenting his compositions. According to Ruthanna Hindes, whose 1946 master's thesis was later published as *George Alfred Townsend, One of Delaware's Outstanding Writers*, Townsend was successful partly because of the speed with which he could produce his compositions, a skill that served him well during his career as a journalist. Hindes also claims that some of his papers were so well written that his teacher thought he had copied them. This allegation again presented itself in his early newspaper work.

In an address forty years later at his alma mater, Townsend shares his credentials as a speaker and praises the school for the education it provided:

> *I have been invited at different times by my native state of Delaware and my parents, the State of Maryland, and by many important bodies to appear before them, but as this High School was the first place where I received a great opportunity, and was allowed to substitute books and study for manual or clerical toil, I feel sometimes as if I had rounded the circle of life on this spot, and here was receiving my Roman Triumph.*

Certainly, it provided the opportunity to discover and develop his talent for writing. It was at Central High School that Townsend met and began to court the girl who would become his wife, "Bessie" Evans Rhodes.

Their courtship was to be a long one, more than five years. Townsend was a persistent suitor and pressed his case quite sincerely and with great conviction. In that era, young men were expected to make their mark in the world, achieve enough success to demonstrate their ability to earn enough money to start families and establish their worthiness as husbands before asking for the hands of their beloveds in marriage.

In one of many long letters to Bessie written in 1857, Townsend is both lovelorn and logical:

> *I am completely exhausted both in mind and hand, for I have composed more than 150 lines of verse since supper, a task of no little magnitude. I have been employed to write the address of the Ledger carriers for New Year and have just finished. Don't you think that I am really in love when I strive to pen you a few lines after the previous exertion? I sincerely hope that you really love me. Just ask yourself the question, "Do I love Alfred Townsend?" Ask yourself the question with unbiased mind, that is free from all prejudice or romance and when you have and when you have answered that ask yourself this second question—"Why do I love him?" Let me have the result of these interrogatories in your next which I hope to get pretty soon. I do not wish to make you suppose that I am one of those sanctimonious fellows who never kissed a girl or played love to anybody. What I meant to say was that I have never confessed or avowed that I loved any girl since I have known you—not that I was never captivated at anytime. Have I never told you that I loved you Bessie: I do, by heaven! by the "might of the stars and angels"—by everything hallowed and revered. I love you with all the devotedness of youth, all the fervor of untrammeled boyhood, all the integrity of one who is too well known to basely endeavor to secure any one's affections for pastime or sport! I will never desert you for another, never will I sell myself to a woman for gold, never will I forsake you unless you request—*
>
> *"Judges and senates have been bought for gold, Esteem and love are never to be sold."*

He was just sixteen years old when he wrote this.

Jealousy—and his denial of such feelings—often appeared in his early letters to Bessie. In 1858, he expresses his passionate and undying love for her but also presents logical arguments to sustain their continued relationship:

> *I will be nineteen when I graduate. It will take me five years at any rate to establish myself in legal practice, and do you think you could love me alone,*

for all that time? Just answer honestly. You profess to be fond of company, you are exceedingly fond of the opposite gender, you court attention and despise books, solitude and sameness.

Do you, knowing that you have such varied failings, still believe that for Alf Townsend alone you could consent to part with visions so entrancing? It will take me years to attain competence. Do you sincerely believe that for five years to come you could discard every proffer, every temptation for me? Just think: wealthier suitors may come, young merchants with splendid homes and…a span of horses, coach, summer house and every pleasure which money may purchase. I have none of these.

With flowery and impassioned words, he implores her to make sure of her choices and to wait patiently until he can claim her. And for the most part, she did, though sometimes not as patiently as he would have liked. His self-professed shyness does not seem to have hindered his outpouring of affection for Bessie. Townsend's letters continue to flow and sometimes seem intended to torment. He describes sights he enjoys in his travels and people he meets. One in particular must have given Bessie pause:

There is a sprightly Irish girl here, who has been travelling on the Continent, and when I have worked pretty hard or worn out the day with visiting and sightseeing, she plays old American tunes for me. I have absolutely taught her to play Yankee Doodle. Fancy that! I am going to visit Ireland for a week or more at Christmas, and she and her Mother have promised to show me the handsomest girls in Dublin.

Their courtship, usually long distance once school ended for them, was rocky at times. Apparently, Bessie gave as good as she was given, for at one point Townsend hears that a very real rival has presented himself to Bessie, while he is not on hand to intervene. In another letter, he defends himself against rumors that have come to Bessie's attention:

The rumor which you recited last evening has operated wonderfully upon my usually easy temper and I hasten to clear my reputation from the slanderous stain which some designing knave has even dared to breathe in woman's ears. Three such stories have been circulated, each implicating me. The first criminated a dear cousin of mine, the second a widow and the third (which is the one to which you allude) a sweet little girl who formerly lived in Cheltenham but has now taken up her home in the distant west.

She is the daughter of a man whose means are limited, but a sweeter child never pressed the green hillside or woke the woodland echoes with her merry laugh. Many a time she has sat upon my knee and often we have wandered together to cull wild flowers by the brooklet's side. I have no proof for mine own innocence save that within which throbs as the heart of a guilty one never throbbed. You may believe such stories if you please, but I will simply ask you—Do you believe that I have the disposition or the villainy toward a girl scarcely fifteen years of age? Trifling I may be, but to such an extent I have never gone.

All this, and they are just sixteen years old. But they were already getting to know each other well, a good basis for an enduring marriage.

Although Townsend was later described as a "self-promoter" (this said with a sniff of disdain to indicate it was not meant to be complimentary), he describes himself in his early years as timid, even writing an essay about it while at school. "The Pleasures of Timidity" does not survive, but it can be assumed he wrote from a position of authority as one who considers himself shy.

A writer by inclination as well as intent, the young Townsend kept a diary, beginning in 1857, titling it *First Year as a New Literary Scribbler, Editor High School Journal, Student of Central High School*. This early journal consisted mostly of his activities with classmates, friends and sometimes poems, notes from textbooks and occasional expenses. The practice of keeping a journal continued throughout most of his life. Later journals also recorded expenses, money received or billed, people encountered and places visited. No doubt he used these for later reference when writing.

He welcomed the attention he received from his writings at school and in the local community, but he was reticent about approaching newspapers for work. It must have come as quite a shock to him when he was asked to become news editor and then editorial writer at the *Philadelphia Inquirer* just as he graduated in 1860. The starting salary was six dollars a week.

He then moved up to reporter, quickly learning the internal workings of newspapers, and by 1861, he was city editor and drama critic for the *Philadelphia Press*. He worked hard and was good at his job but also found time to write poems and a play, *The Bohemians*. It should be noted that then, as now, most reporters aspire to literary careers. Some have successfully made the transition; most have tried only to find, as Townsend later admitted, that it is newspaper work that pays the bills.

Townsend paid his bills with newspaper work and pursued his literary craft with novels, poetry, plays, local history and impressive books on government and other very serious topics. Late in his life, he began to compile an accounting of his articles, stories, columns, addresses and books. It is a list far too long to be published here.

From his days at school and throughout his lengthy career, the speed with which Townsend could write served him well. He was one of the most prolific writers of his, or any, time. For thirty years, he turned out two "letters" a week, in addition to all his other writing endeavors. What are now called stories, articles and commentary were referred to then as letters, hence the name "correspondent." This differentiated the correspondent from a reporter, who primarily covered current events on a daily basis for a local paper.

Later in his career, Townsend wrote or dictated to a secretary and claimed a good day's work to be 1,800 words a day. A comparison to an author of today would be the career of writer William F. Buckley Jr. According to Buckley's son, Christopher, who is still awed by these facts, his father wrote 5,600 of his 700-word columns, and he wrote them in about five minutes, about the time it took to type them. In Townsend's time, columns were much longer, yet in his thirty-year career, he wrote many thousands of them. Buckley claimed to write 1,500 words a day.

For both men, their advantage was that they were constantly circulating in a rich social, political and literary environment, allowing them to absorb considerable amounts of information through osmosis. And they were highly perceptive. Still, Townsend wrote so skillfully, and was so well informed on such a variety of topics, that a certain amount of time must have been spent on interviewing his subjects and researching his topics. Undeniably, by any definition, he was prolific.

2

GEORGE ALFRED TOWNSEND,
WAR CORRESPONDENT

*A*t the outbreak of the Civil War in 1861, Townsend was a reporter at the *Philadelphia Inquirer*. The *New York Herald* hired him to become a correspondent. He was just twenty-one, said to be the youngest correspondent ever sent into the field, but he spent most of that first year in Philadelphia, reporting on how the war was affecting people locally.

In 1862, Townsend was assigned to the Army of the Potomac under General George McClellan and proceeded south to cover an attack on Richmond, Virginia, the capital city of the Confederacy. The attack failed, and Townsend was reassigned to General John Pope, but before the Second Battle of Bull Run, Townsend was seriously ill with Chickahominy fever, an illness thought by some to be similar to malaria. Many of McClellan's troops contracted it when they passed through the swampy and mosquito-infested area near the Chickahominy River. It was also referred to as camp fever, but Townsend does not go into much detail about his symptoms, and he left the war to go to Europe. The illness was fortuitous because it left him able to cover the war at a later day and allowed him a sojourn in Europe. He seems to have recovered quickly enough to make good use of his time in England and Italy, testing the waters for the hoped-for "literary career."

There is no doubt that Townsend took his new job seriously. From a letter to Bessie on leaving:

> *You see, my old friend and flame, therefore that I have cinched it to alienate myself from Philadelphia and my friendships there will necessarily belong to the past. But it does not follow that they are forgotten.*

What is in store for me, I do not know; but I am going to the battlefields
of Virginia to mingle in the romances of camp and carnage. This morning
as I went to leave my stateroom on ship board, I saw a lot of dead men,
boxed and directed to their friends. Thrills of a strange and awful nature
went through me, but I shall become accustomed to such scenes by and by.

Once again, Townsend's ability to write quickly and accurately served him well. Reporting not only on battles won and lost, Townsend captured the many other realities of war with his eye for color and detail. There were many excellent writers who covered the Civil War—John Hay, Henry M. Stanley, Whitelaw Reid, Crosby Noyes, Jerome B. Stillson and Henry Villard, to name a few of the most famous—who went on to lifelong careers in journalism. But many others were merely young adventurers who wrote poorly, sometimes without even being present at the site of the battle. Townsend wrote not only of the fighting but also provided the reader vivid accounts of the things he observed, however unpleasant.

From a dispatch sent to the *New York Herald*:

In many wounds the balls still remained and the discolored flesh was
swollen unnaturally. There were some who been shot in the bowels, and
now and then they were frightfully convulsed, breaking into shrieks and
shouts. Some of them iterated a single word, as "Doctor" or "Help" or
"God" or "Oh!" commencing with a loud spasmodic cry and continuing
the same word till it died away in cadence. The act of calling seemed to
lull the pain. Many were unconscious and lethargic, moving their finger,
and lips mechanically, but never more to open their eyes upon the light: they
were already going through the valley and the shadow.

In a speech more than forty years later at the Central High School in Philadelphia from which he graduated, Townsend describes his service as a correspondent as formative, an opportunity seized and, as he tells us, one that helped secure his place as a journalist:

I remember one such opportunity I had in 1865, near the close of our Civil
War. I had been an army correspondent early in that war, but was confined
to a piece of the army, and subjected to the caprice of petty managers, and
had not the use of my name. Finally, I left the army and went to Europe
and devoted myself to cultivated reading and literary composition for almost
two years. Upon my return, I reluctantly went to the army again, but with

the concession that I should be independent and have my name printed with my work. The desire not to stay, but to go, was my impulsion to see the first great battle, and I was fortunate or fresh enough to obtain from General Sheridan the only account of the battle of Five Forks, the closing and decisive battle of the war at midnight on the first of April, 1865.

Nearly thirty miles separated me from the railway which at six o'clock next morning should take me to the only boat each day down the James River. If I could reach that boat, I would have the exclusive account of that battle printed in New York. But the road was lonely, dangerous and difficult. Yet it was my one opportunity. My horse was so broken down that he could not eat...But if I waited till the morning light that battle would become common property and I set out. The performance gave me a name and settled me in life.

Indeed it did, for Townsend and many others. Aiding that process of recognition was the fact that while Townsend was taking leave from the war in Europe, the Federal government, disturbed by some of the news that was being published regarding the war, ordered publishers to print bylines naming the writers to increase accountability. Townsend took advantage of that, although it is likely that getting a byline was a not a "concession" he won through his own efforts, as he told the audience when speaking at his former high school.

The Federal government took over some newspapers and asked others to stop publishing. Telegraph lines used for communication by the reporters were put under Federal censorship in order to prevent military news from being published. At first, government officials attempted to stop the flood of inaccurate accounts by asking telegraph operators not to send inflammatory reports, but that proved unworkable. They then went to the publishers to ask that accountability be improved by printing reporters' names with their stories.

Seetha Srinivasan, of the University of Chicago Laboratory Middle School, gives this account of reporting on the Civil War:

The Civil War was a very trying time for American newspapers and their reporters. Editors of many newspapers opposed the Lincoln administration's decision to fight to preserve the Union, thereby causing the federal government to take over certain newspapers and asking others to stop publishing. In particular, newspapers from Chicago, Baltimore, and Philadelphia were taken over and operated by federal agents. Despite these restrictive changes made by the government, the newspapers still remained one of the main sources of information. Chicago newspapers were successful in reporting truthfully the battles of the Civil War. Chicago editors and reporters experienced many difficulties, doing their job under the most trying circumstances.

They reported what they saw, sometimes in graphic terms, sometimes detailed, and at other times sketchy. The newspapers of the Civil War period played a very important role in informing people about the happenings at the battlefront. The technology of communication was not as advanced as it is today. In spite of that, the reporters tried hard to give timely reports. They used powerful prose to describe the battles. In contrast, modern-day news is reported rapidly, mostly by television. The images are graphic, and there is no need for eloquent descriptions. Finally, the Civil War journalists practiced very high standards of professional ethics. They were not afraid to tell the truth, and they protected the confidentiality of news sources. The standards established by the Civil War journalists are in practice even today.

Photography was very much present at the battlefield. However, the new technology was not able to capture the action on the battlefield. Sketch artists were still used for newspaper illustrations of the fighting. Thousands of still shots were taken of soldiers and officers, but when battlefields were photographed, it was after the fighting had ended. Many of Mathew Brady's pictures showed battlegrounds littered with the fallen soldiers, sometimes neatly rearranged for the photograph.

At the request of George Smith, publisher of *Cornhill* magazine, Townsend wrote *Campaigns of a Non-Combatant*—stories not only of generals and soldiers but also of people and situations he encountered in his time as a correspondent. This was later republished in 1950 as *Rustics in Rebellion.* Townsend states:

Few wars have been so well chronicled as that now desolating America. Its official narratives have been copious; the great newspapers of the land have been represented in all its campaigns. The pen and the camera have accompanied its bayonets and there probably has not been any skirmish, however insignificant but a score of zealous scribes have remarked and recorded.

With this collection of tales, Townsend attempts to record the war's effect on so many of the ordinary people who were not soldiers, not combatants, but rather unwilling participants in a drama that raged around them and involved them without their consent. He was also skilled at dialogue, and many of these stories are told with dialogue between the characters themselves. His descriptions of his surroundings and the people and conditions he encountered were vividly presented:

> *I am certain that no-body ever felt a tithe of the pain, hunger, heat and weariness which agonized me, when I awoke from a half-hour's sweltering nap. My clothing was soaking with water; I was almost blind; somebody seemed to be sawing a section out of my head; my throat was hot and crackling; my stomach knew all the pangs of emptiness; had scarcely strength to motion away the pertinacious insects. A soldier gave me a trifle of boiling water from his canteen, but I gasped for air; we were living in a vacuum. Sahara would not have been so fierce and burning. Two of us started off to find a spring. We made our way from shade to shade, expiring at every step, and finally, at the base of the hill, on the brink of the swamp, discovered a rill of tepid water that evaporated before it had trickled a hundred yards.*

George Alfred Townsend in his early twenties, looking a bit like Edgar Allan Poe.

At this point, he discovers that his horse is missing and sets out to find him, since a horse is a necessity even for a noncombatant. Locating the horse and its thief, he then had to wrench it loose from its captor and reclaim it for his own use. The life of a correspondent is not an easy one, the one benefit being that he can attend the battles as an observer rather than a participant.

He spent well over a year in Europe, investigating his possibilities and trying various means of making a living with his writing. In 1862, he tried his hand at lectures, and the subject he chose was the one he knew best. At Southport, England, Townsend presented "The Civil War in

George Alfred Townsend, seeming to channel Mark Twain.

America," a topic that was of great interest at that time in England and Western European countries. The presentation offered well-thought-out information on the nature of differences that existed in America and a history of the social and political causes that brought on the terrible separation of the union.

His time was well spent in London and Italy, testing the climate for the literary career he so desired. In Italy, he became intrigued with Giuseppe Garibaldi, the leader of the unification movement there, who was admired by intellectuals and writers in Europe and America. Townsend published a pamphlet about him to be sold in the United States. While in Europe, he no doubt also picked up a degree of sophistication in style and dress that he brought back with him to America.

George Alfred Townsend in Italy, with a bit of Oscar Wilde about him. All three of these photographs were taken within three years and seem to express his yearning to be a writer—or at least look like one.

Of course, in his lectures there were descriptions of the battles he had seen and the people who participated in them. With his talent for observation, he speaks of the formation of the early troops and the differences between the soldiers who opposed one another in battle. Though his bias may seem obvious now, he no doubt thought of his remarks as being merely factual. And much of it is quite true.

The farm boy afield heard the drum and fife going down the road and fell into step awkwardly. The tradesman in the shop became a Captain, the country Justice a Colonel. How oddly walked the shoemaker in shoulder bars and gilt buttons beside the carpenter who flourished pistols and a sword. Everybody hung out the flag, even to the convict who poked it through the prison window, and the number of men, women and boys anxious to die for the country has never been equaled. The best troops came from rural New England, the worst from the populous cities. A few were impressed with the solemnity of the time, but most of the volunteers thought it pleasant frolic and expected to demolish the South as if it were a breakfast.

The South sent her restless and feverish people, many of who had been in service, the filibusters and others in the Comanche and Sioux Wars. The bravo came forth armed with a huge Bowie knife and thirsting for blood; the duelist whose nerve and keen sight had given him a national renown; the slave driver, hard of heart and hand, who swore that he could take his whip and drive every Yankee out of the South.

New England, or Yankee Land, is the most intellectual and vigorous portion of our republic. It has properly been called the brains of America, and the fullest liberty is there tolerated, whether of religion, politics or philosophy. The Yankee is keen at a bargain, but he will return a blow, and although no bully or brawler, maintains what he knows to be his right. One man in every four has volunteered for the war in the six New England states, and that is a greater ratio than is exampled in any states, North or South.

The Southerner is not a scholar, but his instincts and habits are all martial. Something of the hot sun of his section enters into his blood, and his passions are fierce and vehement. He has not patience, for this is a virtue wrought out by hard toil, and labor is not honorable in the South. He is quick to strike, for that is a lesson in the slaveholder's primer, and accomplished: for him, knifing and dueling are institutions. Military organization is indispensable to these people, for they know the treachery of the servile race they call their slaves.

Returning from Europe in 1865, Townsend resumed coverage of the war and had the good fortune to interview General Phillip Sheridan just after the decisive battle at Five Forks in Virginia. He was the first to submit a dispatch on this very important event, and this scoop launched his career. After the war, his investigative reporting and writing on Lincoln's assassination put him further on the path to fame and fortune. He was able to stay on that path for many years, although during the war, he spent relatively little time in the battlefield arena.

3

George Alfred Townsend Marries and Becomes GATH

*I*n December 1865, Townsend married Bessie Evans Rhodes of Philadelphia. They had been sweethearts for almost eight years, on and off perhaps, but neither seems to have had any other serious relationship during that time. He had sufficiently established himself to take a wife and begin a family.

After the wedding, in 1866, the Townsends went to Europe. He could be impetuous, but he was also given to careful planning and continued to pursue career opportunities and expand the scope of his writing while in Europe. Their first child, Genevieve Madeleine, was born in Paris in October 1866.

In 1867, the Townsends had settled in Washington, D.C., a suitable base of operations given Townsend's strong interest in government and politics. Life was hectic, exciting and filled with the competition and deadlines of the newspapermen who gathered there, and Townsend thrived on it. It was the perfect setting for an ambitious writer with talent and drive who was intent on building a successful career.

By this time, Townsend had resolved to become an independent journalist, writing in-depth, well-informed and lengthy pieces, as well as longer works. Besides being immersed in the day-to-day business of government in Washington, he wrote books on the subject: *The New World Compared with the Old: A Description of the American Government, Institutions, and Enterprises, and of Those of Our Great Rivals at the Time, Particularly England and France* in 1869; *Washington Inside and Outside* in 1873; and *Events at the National Capital and the Campaign of 1876.*

An early photo of GATH and Bessie, probably after their marriage.

Townsend had no desire to harness his inquisitive and adventurous spirit to an editor's arbitrary assignments. Although being an independent meant that he would have to market his own work, it also meant that his prodigious output earned him far better remuneration than that of a salaried reporter. And, as most newspapermen do, he longed to be literary, to write important works that would outlive the fleeting fame of news writing, forgotten as soon as the next day's newspaper appeared.

It was during this time that George Alfred Townsend became GATH, the nom de plume under which he wrote most of his published newspaper work and by which he was known to an increasingly vast readership. He created it by using the first letter of each of his names, and adding an "H" at the end. Gath explained that it derives from a Bible verse (as the son of a preacher, he was very familiar with the Bible): "Tell it not in Gath, publish it not in the streets of Askelon, lest the daughters of the Philistines rejoice." Some jokester was reputed to have asked, "Does the H stand for heaven or hell?" and was told that most who knew him would answer the latter.

There were other pen names, perhaps as many as twenty on various works: Swede, Finn, Johnny Bouquet and Laertes. Those names sometimes found their way into his stories, and Askelon became the name of his first summer home, the first house in what became a large estate in Western Maryland.

Throughout his long career, he demonstrated the huge and diverse range of his knowledge and his writing skills. He read voraciously, adding to his store of knowledge. His constant quest for knowledge led him to read widely and to acquire a huge library consisting of more than five thousand books.

As was the custom of educated men of his era, he was familiar with the classics, with ancient Greek and Latin mythology and with history. His writing is peppered with references to these events and characters, mythological or real, and he wrote about them without pretension or pomposity but with familiarity as though they were personal acquaintances or stored in a mental reference catalogue to be used as needed to make a certain point.

There are conflicting reports of GATH's personality. Before he was thirty, he had experienced life in Europe, on the battlefield and as a husband and father. Hindes describes him as "modest, unassuming, and hated the so-called 'social climber.' So modest was he of his own successes in life that it was not until after his death when the newspapers from all over the country printed his obituary column that his grandson, Mr. George Alfred Bonaventure, fully realized the scope and importance of his literary career."

Later, Hindes mentions his many speaking engagements at social gatherings but insists that "in spite of his fame he had no natural or affected signs of his vocation. He was honest and independent. He was never what could be called a worldly person, and although he was educated, he was not conceited."

An unnamed female correspondent with a Boston paper describes him in more detail, but not unflatteringly:

> *The next minute I am shaking hands with the most notable correspondent of the city, for it is "Gath" of the* Philadelphia Times, *"Laertes" of the* Graphic—*George Alfred Townsend himself!*
>
> *He is tall and finely formed, and the face is a study; the laughing eyes are near together; the forehead gives little hint of the active grain it hides; the brown hair is thick and slightly wavy, and the mouth an exceedingly pleasant one.*
>
> *He sits down, chatting in such happy fashion that you find yourself saying all sorts of things and forgetting that if it will serve his purpose you may be served up in his next paragraph, 'till you remember it with a gasp and review your utterances to see how you have been talking. You understand at once the way in which he gathers information. He is by no means a friend of the paper and notebook order; he doesn't seem to be paying any special attention; he trifles with his cane and you would never guess that he would remember every word you have spoken.*

Did he have a special aspect of his personality reserved for women?

Others remember him quite differently. A display in the museum first created in the 1970s by the Department of Natural Resources in Gathland State Park described him as "feisty, egotistical, full of himself" and a "self-promoter." An article in the *Washington Evening Star* presents an example of GATH's more combative side:

> *Mr. Walker, of the* Chicago Times *Looks for "GATH" and Finds Him.*
>
> *One Walker, the Washington Correspondent of the* Chicago Times, *who for sometime past has been engaged in the business of libeling public men, private ladies, and his brother correspondents received a severe castigation this morning at the hands of Mr. George Alfred Townsend. The affair took place at one of the newspaper offices in 14ᵗʰ Street, in which Mr. Townsend and Walker accidentally met, and was caused by a statement forwarded to the* Chicago Times *by Walker, to the effect that Townsend lives in a house given to him by the "Washington ring" to purchase his commendation. Mr. Townsend, on encountering Walker this morning, charged him with writing the falsehood, at the same time saying that when he (Walker) came to Washington, he (Townsend) had*

befriended him, and that his kindness has been repaid by an infamous libel upon him.

Walker, wincing under this onslaught, said he was "looking for him," Townsend, yesterday, as he wanted to have a talk with him, and added that he received the information which he sent to the Times *from his (Townsend's) office. Mr. Townsend thereupon called him a liar, and seizing Walker's umbrella, followed it up with a number of vigorous blows. Walker grasped the umbrella and began to retreat, when Mr. Townsend struck him a number of times with his fist, fetching the claret, which flowed copiously.*

It would probably have gone hard for Walker had it not been for Mr. James Holland, of the Associated Press, who happened to be present and who, assuming the role of peace maker, separated the combatants, thus saving further effusion of blood. Walker was severely punished and Townsend escaped untouched. Walker probably concludes that "Gath" is capable of vigorous hitting from the shoulder as well as with the pen.

GATH was highly respected as a writer and was also in demand as a lecturer, an important source of income for him. Once he educated himself on the wide range of subjects he wrote about, he could sell it again on the lecture circuit. In the days before radio and TV, lectures were a popular and educational form of entertainment. And GATH had plenty to talk about.

The Civil War brought new energy to Washington, D.C. New arrivals— young and generally inexperienced—flooded the city to set up shop, selling their dispatches to whomever would buy. They were unabashedly Northern sympathizers and so thickly clustered around 14th Street near the Willard Hotel that the stretch became known as Newspaper Row.

By 1870, GATH was a player in the postwar newspaper world, known nationally to readers and a respected member of "The Row," Washington's journalistic epicenter. Among the many well-known journalists living there was Mark Twain. He and Townsend at one time lived in the same boarding house and remained on good terms throughout their careers.

In 1871, Twain and GATH were photographed, along with David Gray, an editor at the *Buffalo Courier*, at Mathew Brady's studio. The picture illustrates GATH's development socially as well as professionally. All three gentlemen are casual and confident, sure of their places in the world, or at least in their own arena. Clearly, they are the Young

George Alfred Townsend, Samuel Clemens and David Gray in Mathew Brady's Washington, D.C. studio. This photograph was taken after the Civil War, long before Mark Twain began wearing white suits and when his hair was quite dark. Townsend is wearing a rose in his buttonhole, and David Gray, a reporter for the *Courier*, wears gloves, typical of the Victorian era. *Courtesy of the Library of Congress*

Turks of their day. GATH's attire in the photograph seems an attempt at formality, yet the flower is awkwardly holding his jacket together, and his exposed vest is peculiarly puckered. GATH is only thirty years old but seems to feel he is at the top of his game, with good times still to come.

On his thirty-fifth birthday, he celebrated in Washington by giving a breakfast at Welcker's to a number of personal friends, among whom were Justice Miller, of the United States Supreme Court; Senator Henry Anthony, of Rhode Island; Mr. Horace White; Colonel George B. Corkhill; and Mr. Crosby S. Noyes.

This article appeared in the paper, reporting on the event:

> *Mr. Townsend has been so prolific and graphic a writer and his name has been so constantly before the public for some fifteen years, that most people doubtless have supposed him to be a gray-haired veteran and it will therefore be a genuine surprise to them to learn that he is but thirty-five, with not a hair of his abundant raven locks turned gray, and that he has hardly reached the full maturity of his brilliant powers as a journalist, and poet as well. Since he commenced his singularly active literary career, writing books, contributing to magazines, and keeping up at the same time the most readable of correspondence for half a dozen newspapers, he has doubtless been the most quoted of any American writer, hence the familiarity of the public with his name. And he looks as if he might keep things up for half a centennial, at least.*

GATH had few peers who could match his prodigious output, but there is considerable confusion about exactly how much he could produce, especially regarding his newspaper work. Several sources claim he wrote two columns a day for an assortment of newspapers. Even if the same column went to all of those papers, it would mean that he must have produced ten columns a week, and these would have been lengthy and detailed works. It is very difficult to believe he could have done more than two a week, as stated in other sources, considering the fact that these articles had to be researched, interviews conducted and travel time included. And his other writing—books, poems, lectures and public appearances—must have consumed considerable time and energy.

However, in 1891, when Townsend was fifty years old, *Lippincott's* published an article called "An Interviewer Interviewed: A Talk with GATH." The interviewer is not named, and the format seems suspiciously like a ploy GATH used to talk about himself without being subjected to questions he would not have wanted to answer. In response to a question posed by the "interviewer" on how much he had written and published, he says, "I have not written less than two columns a day for thirty-five years, or four thousand words a day, making a total of more than fifty millions of words."

He claimed that:

> *the attempt to supply four or five different papers at once with hand-written manuscript was destroying my nervous organization. By 1867, I found that I could dictate, at first to long-hand and afterwards to short-hand writers; and for about twenty three years I have talked nearly the whole of*

*my correspondence, though I find it a rest now and then to pick up the pen
and write three thousand to four thousand words.*

In a letter to Bessie, GATH takes credit for 1,800 words on a good day.
It seems doubtful that he could manage that many columns over a period
of thirty-five years. And as previously noted, William F. Buckley, the most
prolific of writers, claimed 1,500 words a day. Finally, to further confuse the
issue, a permanent marker at the Gathland Park proclaims that he wrote
18,000 words a day—an obvious typographical error, but there it is.

4

His Writing Styles Are Many and Varied

*W*ith his regular columns appearing in papers all over the country, in major cities like Boston, Baltimore, New York, Chicago, Cleveland, Washington, San Francisco, St. Louis and Cincinnati, GATH was widely read, and his self-syndication made him a wealthy man, by newspaper standards.

As GATH himself often admitted, he made his money writing for newspapers. His columns, or "letters," as they were called then, appeared all over the country. With perhaps thousands of these produced over a period of thirty-five years, it is impossible to list the topics he covered.

Still, his desire to burn brightly as a writer of literature continued and fueled the writing of his more scholarly and analytical works on government and politics. GATH also put his pen to other kinds of writing. The range of his subject matter, and his diverse styles of writing, was staggering. It seems there is nothing he didn't attempt.

So prolific was he that there are hundreds of examples of the various kinds of literature he wrote, far too many even to list, or in some cases count, as some of what he wrote was never published and has since disappeared. Choosing just a few categories, brief selections are provided to introduce some of these styles.

Folklore

Folklore was among the first efforts of his literary attempts. *Tales of the Chesapeake*, published in 1880, is a collection of poems and stories written over a period of time and collected for publication. It contains stories of locals, mostly residents of the Chesapeake locale of the title, and some of the stories are told as poems. The book was the result of a trip to the Eastern Shore when GATH was thirty-five and wanted to revisit these recollections of his childhood. *Tales of the Chesapeake* reached back into his childhood on Maryland's Eastern Shore, with stories about the people who lived in these still-rural Chesapeake Bay waterfront settings. *Tales* and other quasi-fictional books allowed him to use the full range of his descriptive ability to describe the unique beauty and culture of the area and his talent for dialogue, bringing the local folk to life.

In this genre, he also enjoyed using dialect: Eastern Shore watermen, Southerners of all stripes, Appalachian farmers, Negroes and others native to his stories. The modern reader soon finds himself befuddled, struggling through the dialects much as Br'er Rabbit's readers tried to claw their way through the briar patch. Whether he thought he was preserving the dialects for history, or whether he just thought they added color and texture to his stories, is not known. It was probably a bit of both.

Growing up on the Delmarva Peninsula, GATH observed the ways of the natives of the area and wrote about them in *Tales of the Chesapeake*. The publisher describes it as "a series of weird yet genial and powerful legends coined out of the author's mind, blending the tenderness of Hans Anderson with the ingenuity of Poe, and the light and shade of Hawthorne." He goes on to say that the dramatic element of these tales is

"OUR TENDEREST TALE-TELLER:

Tales of the Chesapeake.

BY
GEO. ALFRED TOWNSEND,
"GATH."
PRICE - - $1.25.

An advertising flier for *Tales of the Chesapeake*, Townsend's recollections of the Eastern Shore of Maryland.

extraordinary, "and the pure crystal English of the style is never sacrificed by the fine imagination. A pleasing well of humor rises through the *Tales*, which are far from local in their interest, but signify the cosmopolitan and scholar as well as the antiquarian."

He begins with a lyrical passage:

> *A fruity smell is in the school-house lane; The clover bees are sick with evening heats; A few old houses from the window-pane fling back the flame of sunset, and there beats the throb of oars from basking oyster fleets, And clangorous music of the oyster tongs plunged down in deep bivalvulous retreats, And sound of seine drawn home with negro songs.*

Some of the stories in *Tales* are actually poems, written, as all of his poetry was, in rhyming couplets. Here are two stanzas from a story about Funkstown, far from the Chesapeake Bay, closer to the place where GATH eventually built his Frederick County estate:

> *Nick Hammer sat in Funkstown before his tavern door*
> *The same old blue-stone tavern the wagoners knew of yore,*
> *When the Conestoga schooners came staggering under their load,*
> *And the lines of slow pack-horses*
> *Stamped over the National Road.*
> *"The Funks is all up-country"—That's all I could think to say,*
> *There never was Funks in Funkstown, and there ain't any Funks to-day.*
> *"Why man," he says, "the city that stands on Potomac's shores*
> *Was settled by Funk, the elder, who afterward settled yours!"*

The use of dialect was not meant to disparage the characters but to identify the place in which the story happened and familiarize the reader with that locale. In an excerpt from *Crutch, the Page*, the reader is taken to Texas, where people probably did speak this way:

> *The Honorable Jeems Bee, of Texas, sitting in his committee-room half an hour before the convening of Congress, waiting for his negro familiar to compound a julep, was suddenly confronted by a small boy on crutches.*
>
> *"A letter!" exclaimed Mr. Bee, "with the frank of Reybold on it—that Yankeest of Pennsylvania Whigs! Yer's familiarity! Wants me to appoint one U—U—U, what?"*

"*Uriel Basil,*" *said the small boy on crutches, with a clear, bold, but rather sensitive voice.*

"*Uriel Basil, a page in the House of Representatives, bein' an infirm, deservin' boy, willin' to work to support his mother. Infirm boy wants to be a page, on the recommendation of a Whig, to a Dimmycratic committee. I say, gen'lemen, what do you think of that, heigh?*"

This last addressed to some other members of the committee, who had meantime entered.

"*Infum boy will make a spry page,*" *said the Hon. Box Izard, of Arkansaw.*

"*Harder to get infum page than the Speaker's eye,*" *said the orator, Pontotoc Bibb, of Georgia.*

"*Harder to get both than a 'pintment in these crowded times on a opposition recommendation when all ole Virginny is yaw to be tuk care of,*" *said Hon. Fitzchew Smy, of the Old Dominion.*

The small boy standing up on crutches, with large hazel eyes swimming and wistful, so far from being cut down by these criticisms, stood straighter, and only his narrow little chest showed feeling, as it breathed quickly under his brown jacket.

"*I can run as fast as anybody,*" *he said impetuously.* "*My sister says so. You try me!*"

"*Who's yo' sister, bub?*"

"*Joyce.*"

"*Who's Joyce?*"

"*Joyce Basil—Miss Joyce Basil to you, gentlemen. My mother keeps boarders. Mr. Reybold boards there. I think it's hard when a little boy from the South wants to work, that the only body to help him find it is a Northern man. Don't you?*"

Novels

His first novel, *The Entailed Hat*, published in 1884, is called a "romance," though its protagonist is Patty Cannon, a thoroughly evil character, who ran an underground slave trafficking operation. She was a real person, though already a legend in GATH's time, and she was completely ruthless. Patty's gruesome operations were actually a backdrop for the romance that was carried on by younger, quite innocent and very brave characters. In this excerpt from chapter twenty-four, we see GATH's ability to use dialogue to tell the story and dialect to bring definition to the characters:

In them days they didn't kidnap much; it was jest a-beginnin'. The war of '12 busted everything on the bay, burned half a dozen towns, kept the white men layin' out an' watchin', and made loafers of half of 'em, an' brought bad volunteers an' militia yer to trifle with the porer gals, an' some of them strangers stuck yer after the war was done. I don't know whar ole Ebenezer come from; some says this, an' some that. All we know is, that he an' the Hanlen gals, one of 'em Patty Cannon, was the head devils in an' after the war....

The British begun to run the black people off in the war. The black people wanted to go to 'em. The British filled the islands in Tangier yer with nigger camps; they was a goin' to take this whole peninsuly, an' collect an' drill a nigger army on it to put down Amerikey. When the war was done, the British sailed away from Chesapeake Bay with thousands of them colored folks, an' then the people yer begun to hate the free niggers.

They hated free niggers as if they was all Tories an' didn't love Amerikey. So, seein' the free niggers hadn't no friends, these Johnsons an' Patty Cannon begun to steal 'em, by smoke! There was only a million niggers in the whole country; Louisiana was a-roarin' for 'em; every nigger was wuth twenty horses or thirty yokes of oxen, or two good farms around yer, an' these kidnappers made money like smoke, bought the lawyers, went into polytics, an' got sech a high hand that they tried a murderin' of the nigger traders from Georgey an' down thar, comin' yer full of gold to buy free people. That give 'em a back-set, an' they hung some of Patty's band—some at Georgetown, some at Cambridge.

An article appeared in the *Baltimore Sun*, written by Anthony Smith. He shares a comment from an 1891 review of *The Entailed Hat*. The reviewer, Levin L. Waters, a resident of Somerset County, where the book is set, was not a fan:

It is true that he has gotten hold of some of the traditions of this locality, but he has perverted them to improper uses and his book is calculated to create very false impressions of the community, its people and their social status.

His book is trash, and to my mind written in a spiteful mood toward the upper class of this peninsula in revenge for the exclusiveness by which the author was shut out.

A ROMANCE OF THE
DELAWARE PENINSULA AND THE EAST-
ERN SHORE OF MARYLAND.

Harper & Brothers have just ready Mr. George Alfred
Townsend's ("Gath") social and historical tale, entitled:

THE ENTAILED HAT;

OR, PATTY CANNON'S TIMES,

a volume of 575 pages (16mo, Cloth, $1 50), the theme
of which is of deep interest to every citizen of Maryland,
Delaware, Eastern Virginia, and, it may be added, to
every scion of old colonial families in every part of the
country. It is a romance, vivid, weird, and picturesque,
founded on the rise of modern society upon the ruins of
the colonial and revolutionary aristocracy, in the states

An advertisement for his most popular novel, *The Entailed Hat*, which featured
Patty Cannon, who kidnapped free blacks and sold them into slavery. She lived
long before Townsend but came down to him as legend during his childhood.

43

A favorite ploy GATH frequently used was mixing fact with fiction. In the excerpt above, he gives us a bit of a history lesson, explaining how this business venture came about and why it was successful for those who did it. Later, in *Katy of Catoctin*, he uses John Wilkes Booth to similar advantage. Booth finds himself among the rustics in Western Maryland and courts Nelly Harbaugh, who is already engaged to a suitable young man in her community. Nelly is tempted but regains her senses and rejects Booth. He then apologizes for his attempted seduction, admitting that she is better off not to have chosen him. Given GATH's feelings about Booth's assassination of President Lincoln, it would appear that he has treated Booth rather kindly in the story. The following is excerpted from the author's preface to *Katy of Catoctin*:

> *From the hour the author stood by the dead face of Abraham Lincoln, in the Executive Mansion at Washington, he has had the idea of writing a romance upon the conspiracy of Booth.*
>
> *Like many such literary projects nursed by a journalist, this one had not only to be postponed, but finally to become a portion of a broader story, because too many of the actors in the tragedy still lived, and the mere crime presented no elevated moral to justify its embellishment.*
>
> *He felt that, while to have written this book earlier would have been to speak too harshly and too narrowly of some agents in the crime, to postpone the composition longer would have been to remand it to mere antiquarian literature and lose the missionary use and the heartiness of adventure; for, when he knew Booth personally and saw his associates executed, the author was turning into twenty-five, and, when he unraveled the skein of Booth's concealment and flight after the crime, the author was turning forty-four years. Voters had grown up in the interim who had been but tottling babes when the mighty war ceased with this sacrificial mass, and the President's death ended the wild Maryland epic, of which the raid of John Brown, the Baltimore riots, Antietam battle, and the spy system in the old Potomac counties were elements.*
>
> *Enough of all this was yet undiscovered to leave space for fancy to enliven the athletic game, and in one or two cases characters have been wholly invented, or rather made out of general types and conditions, to replace others not proper to be copied.*
>
> *The author not only lived contemporary with the personages of his book, but he was an active traveler and sightseer with and among them. No natural scene is sketched in this book that did not dwell upon his sight, and he trusts that the impassioned scenes of action have been tinted in subordination to a national and human philosophy.*

The Life, Crime and Capture of John Wilkes Booth was a kind of hybrid: investigative reporting that later became a book. GATH was passionate about this project, and his coverage of Lincoln's assassination, and the conspiracy that spawned it, added to his growing reputation.

He had met Booth years earlier, when he was drama critic for the *Philadelphia Inquirer*, and had spoken to him briefly in Washington, D.C., just weeks before Lincoln was killed, but the detail in his writing on Booth's life and personality and the anecdotes were acquired through his own research.

Later, his articles were gathered into a pamphlet and sold without his permission. GATH confronted the publisher and was paid $300 for the rights. Much later, the story was fictionalized in his novel *Katy of Catoctin.*

POETRY

GATH wrote poetry during his entire lifetime, probably more of it than any other literary genre. It did not provide much income. His subject matter and styles varied, as they did in his other writing, but one thing was consistent: all his poems, long and short, were written in rhyming couplets. From flowery declarations of love and devotion in florid Victorian excess to what can only be called battle anthems, they shared another trademark of his style. References to ancient history, mythology and literature were scattered like stars in the night sky through the verses. Certainly, some of this was meant to demonstrate his familiarity with all these topics, but it also was natural for him to embellish some of his heartfelt work with allusions to classic expression.

Some of his poetry reads like ballads, stories of courage or hardship or woeful lament, others like anthems of heroic battle. And still others read like odes to some virtue or a beloved person or place, but all are presented in rhyming couplets.

Here are the beginning few lines of a poem called "The Press":

> *Columbus seeing through the lambent air*
> *The world he imagined basking virgin there,*
> *Felt not the blushes youthful cheeks that tint*
> *To see their compositions first in print*
> *How large, how bold, how wonderful, how terse,*
> *And what a printer that could set such verse!*
> *Sure all have seen it, from our sweetheart down,*

Still do we print still thrilling o'er the boon,
Like fondness lasting after honeymoon,
Until we see a road on either hand,
Open before us and to heaven expand;
One wide and dusty, crowded by the herd,
The other travelled by the singing bird;
One like a river by a navy shook;
The other like a pathway up a brook;
One endless, shelterless, contentious rude;
The other green with shade and solitude;
Still do they seem not far apart to tend,
And glide together ere they reach the end.
One is The Press. Try that! It must insure
A crossing over into Literature.

He continues, for an astounding 120 lines, all rhyming couplets, to tell the story of a newsman. And although the majority of his readers might not have been of sufficient erudition to understand all of them, he brings in supporters from various centuries, including a pharaoh, Phaeton and Apollo, William Brownlow, William Tell, Sam Houston, David Farragut, William Shakespeare, James Boswell, Samuel Johnson, Francis Bacon and even Thomas Edison.

In another lament, "Salt River" (and there were many of these epic works), he holds forth for 170 lines to tell of conflict and death, with sorrow, despair and sadness.

NEWSPAPERS

It is in his newspaper work—his daily columns—that his wit and wisdom come through to the reader even today, and this explains the long-lasting appeal he had for his readers.

Some of his columns were in the style of reporting, others profiled individuals, still others were of projects undertaken by various people and many were well-reasoned commentary of social issues of the time. Many were just a sort of newsy, sometimes gossipy record of people's comings and goings, debunking myths and rumors and generally writing about whatever he came upon that interested him.

A snippet from one column gets into the Barbara Fritchie legend. Fritchie was a friend of Francis Scott Key, and they participated in a memorial service for George Washington in Frederick, where Fritchie lived. According to legend, at the age of ninety-five, she waved a Union flag at Stonewall Jackson's troops as they passed through Frederick in the Maryland Campaign. The story was immortalized by John Greenleaf Whittier's poem of 1864, which begins:

> *"Shoot, if you must, this old gray head,*
> *But spare your country's flag," she said.*
> *A shade of sadness, a blush of shame,*
> *Over the face of the leader came;*
> *The nobler nature within him stirred*
> *To life at that woman's deed and word;*
> *"Who touches a hair of yon gray head*
> *Dies like a dog! March on!" he said.*

The story was not at all true, and GATH writes of a Mrs. Southworth, whom he appears to have admired, and tells us: "When Mrs. Southworth was told of this fiction, she replied, 'Well, if it did not occur, it ought to have done so.'" He writes:

> *Mrs. Southworth lives on a steep hill street in Georgetown, and rattles off her peculiar fictions at the rate of twelve or fifteen columns a week. Some time ago she was taken with small-pox, and all the while the ulcers were hideously running all over her face, she hired a manager and plunged into the labyrinths of a serial romance. She makes six thousand dollars a year, has engagements offered or pending in London and Paris, has spent two years in Europe and has educated her children handsomely and is a native of this district or of the adjoining part of Maryland.*

In the same column, he notes that "at Hartford the other day, I saw Gideon Wells sitting at dinner at the Alleyn House, looking like a bleached billy-goat, as usual. I was sorry to learn that Gideon comes back to Hartford richer than when he departed."

Lectures

GATH was highly respected as a writer and was also in demand as a lecturer, an important source of income for him. Once educated on the wide range of subjects he wrote about, he could sell his knowledge again on the lecture circuit. In the days before radio and then TV, lectures were a popular and educational entertainment. And GATH had plenty to talk about.

While he was usually well received, as he reports to Bessie in his letters to her, he sometimes encountered a negative reaction from reviewers. This is an excerpt from a review in the *Palladium* when he appeared before a Richmond audience:

> *George Alfred Townsend appeared before a very respectable audience at Phillips Hall Wednesday evening last.*
>
> *We attended with the expectation of hearing something worthy of the high position the lecturer assumes to occupy as a literary man of vast means and scope.*
>
> *But it was a dismal utter failure on every count by which such a thing can be measured by any savage or civilized human. We do not recollect ever sitting so long under a similar raining down of misty adjectives and desperate efforts at making sky-scraping oratory out of such windy nothingness. The announced subject was "Lands to the North of Us."*
>
> *Townsend appeared before the Richmond audience, book in hand, and commenced reading, turning over a new leaf every ten or fifteen words or so...and gesticulating with the other hand, at the same time keeping up a perpetual see-sawing of his body from right to left, like a pendulum we all wished would stop.*
>
> *Pure drivel! What ideas, fancies or impressions the reader wished to awaken in the hearts and minds of his hearers would be hard to guess at... By far the silliest feature of the whole sorry performance consisted in his repeating all the ephemeral data to be found in the history of the world that would bore the teeth out of anyone's head. He appeared to have carefully collected all this trite information single handedly and is now chirping it around the county after the popular stylings of a minstrel, but instead of a banjo being plucked, he uses his mouth.*
>
> *It is a good thing we were not armed! Is there a tree high enough in all of the county for him to dangle from? Near the end Townsend dropped the book from his left hand and went off into a genuine pleasurable paroxysm of eloquence by stating: "Our manifest destiny is hemispherical! Clasping*

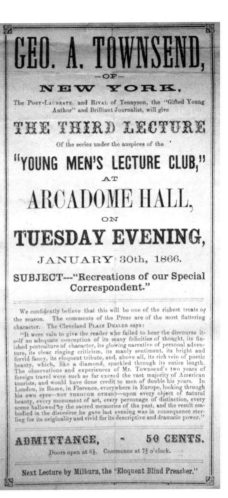

Right: An advertisement for Townsend's 1866 lecture "Recreations of our Special Correspondent." It describes him as "Poet Laureate, Rival of Tennyson, A Gifted young Author and Brilliant Journalist."

Below: A political cartoon featuring Townsend (center). It is not known what political issue the cartoon was meant to illustrate, but it shows that Townsend was part of the ongoing political drama.

the continent in our arms we will plant the stars and stripes upon the two poles, generate our own electricity and mix our own thunder!"

Perhaps this speaks of a facet of his personality that developed apace with his growing renown and became the genesis of comments from those who found him pompous, ostentatious and longwinded. Or perhaps the grandiosity of his words is more easily digested in print, when portions might be skipped.

Townsend was adept at reporting and even more skilled at artful description, which served him well throughout his career. From a 1907 article about GATH by W.R. Hamilton in the *Baltimore Sun*, Sir Henry Stanley writes in a letter with a $100 contribution for the War Correspondents Arch GATH would later build:

> *"I am glad to know," said the man who found Livingstone, "that you still keep your pen occupied, for I greatly honor that pen. At one time it was one of the most envied things on earth to me. There was such verve and uplifting power in its grand, rolling lines as it described in unequaled style the shock of battle and the thunder of war. Every scene you touched upon stood out boldly, as it were from the page. There were giants in those days, the days of my youth, but you bore the palm for splendid descriptive writing."*
>
> *The opinion of Stanley was that of hundreds of thousands of others, and the opportunity to publish correspondence over the famous signature, "GATH" became one which newspaper editors eagerly sought. He applied to the exposition of current events a wonderful knowledge of the byways, as well as of the highways of history and literature. When opinions were to be expressed he never sugar-coated them. He was not given to fencing with a buttoned rapier, but to dealing blows with a two-handed sword.*

While he may not have been universally loved, he definitely had enough variety in his writing to build a huge following, if not for his poems, then for his political writing, his folklore or his columns. Two admirers whose names are still recognized today sent letters of praise for *Tales of the Chesapeake*:

Hartford, Feb. 26
My dear Friend—
> *Many thanks for the book. I got it yesterday evening and gave it a chance toward bedtime, but it failed to put me to sleep or even make me drowsy. Few books treat me so unkindly. I read it more than half through, picking*

out the plums, such as "The Big Idiot," "The Circuit Preacher," etc., and greatly enjoyed the entertainment. Thank you again. I will respond when my book comes out, George Alfred.

Your friend
(signed) Sl. L. Clemens (Mark Twain)

Cambridge, Feb. 25, 1880
My dear Sir,
I am much obliged to you for your Tales of the Chesapeake. *If the book is an "oyster shell" as you are pleased to term it in your letter, it is one, I am sure, that has pearls in it; I have already found: "Herman of Bohemia Manor" and "Old St. Mary's."*
Thanks, many thanks,

Yours very truly,
(signed) Henry W. Longfellow

By any reckoning, his "letters" or columns, which appeared in newspapers across the country for thirty-five years, were far more popular than his books or poetry. It was this kind of work that made him famous and paid his bills. Still, he longed for recognition as a writer of literature, of the kind that he himself admired most ardently.

Many thousands across the country were avid readers of his column. Its wide and long-lasting appeal is explained by an author called "Savoyard" in the *Washington Star*, printed in 1911 on the occasion of his seventieth birthday:

For many years I read "GATH" daily, and what an abundant wealth of information and suggestion were his wares! His discursive style always fascinated and occasionally bewildered. He seemed to know everything and could give the source of his information. He appeared to know everybody and who was everybody's daddy and who everybody's mamma. He took captive his readers, and for years he was the leading correspondent of the American Newspaper press.

As reported by Hindes in her thesis on Townsend: "He was a walking encyclopedia and could talk intelligently on almost any subject mentioned. What he found he did not know, he made it his business to learn." And it was that passion that inspired the library he established at Gapland.

5

HAVING FOUND SUCCESS,
HE NOW SEEKS REFUGE FROM IT

*G*ATH often expressed the writer's need to remove himself from the fray. He states that in 1865 and 1866, he lectured on two hundred nights and made arrangements with the *Chicago Tribune*, the *Cleveland Leader*, the *Cincinnati Commercial*, the *Missouri Democrat* and other papers to submit columns. The following is from an article that appeared in the *Cincinnati Enquirer*:

> *After I became more and more busy and commenced Washington correspondence in 1867, I found that to run a few hundred miles away was a medical relief every now and then. In 1874, I removed to New York City and lived there fifteen years, but the regular round of city promenades, dinners, clubs, bad weather and want of exercise and of original material caused me to make journeys every few weeks, often to places where my incentive had been the library.*
>
> *I would think, for instance, that I knew very little about Monroe's administration, and to get Monroe near at hand would go to see his house in Virginia, and after that every incident in his life seemed to be vitalized. I would feel a curiosity about James Buchanan and would go and talk to his neighbors at Lancaster, Penn. These journeys seldom were more than sixty hours long, but they became finally as necessary to keep up my industry as the colchicum pill is to the gouty man.*

By 1870, GATH was a celebrated journalist, writing columns, "letters," books, poetry, commentary and news. After the publication in 1865 of *The

Life, Crime and Capture of John Wilkes Booth (a collection of articles he had written on the subject), *Campaigns of a Non-Combatant* (1866), *The Life and Battles of Garibaldi and His March on Rome* (1867), *The New World Compared with the Old* (1869), *Lost Abroad* (an 1870 book similar to Mark Twain's *Innocents Abroad*) and numerous pamphlets in addition to his regular work, he was very busy.

In his personal life, GATH and Bessie had suffered the loss of a daughter, Ella, in 1873 and Donn Piatt, who was three years old when he died in 1875. Finally, in 1841, George Alfred was born. Both he and his older sister, Genevieve, survived to adulthood. His brother, Stephen Emory Townsend, died in Nicaragua in 1856. His mother, Mary Milbourne Townsend, died in 1868. His brother

An autographed photograph of Townsend, signed "Gath."

Ralph Milbourne Townsend, who had become a physician, died in 1877, at the age of thirty-two.

In 1874, apparently needing a change, GATH moved his family to New York City. He said he had moved to Washington to write about government, and in New York he would focus on learning more about financial matters. Though there may have been other reasons that prompted the move, that was his stated motive. The family lived there for fourteen years, returning to Washington in 1889.

In 1884, while GATH was on his way through Western Maryland to Harpers Ferry, doing research for the novel that would become *Katy of Catoctin*, he became acquainted with Crampton's Gap. Crampton's was one of the three gaps in the South Mountain that had seen battle during the Civil War more than twenty years earlier, and these battles were the prelude to the Battle of Antietam that took place just three days later. He was impressed with the beauty and the historical significance of the site and purchased the land.

On September 14, 1862, Crampton's Gap was one of three gaps (along with Fox's Gap and Turner's Gap) in South Mountain that gave troops access to Harpers Ferry, Sharpsburg, Hagerstown and Boonsboro. A series of delaying actions, referred to as the Battle of South Mountain, cost Lee his initiative in the Maryland Campaign. However important these battles might have been, they were quickly overshadowed when troops converged for the horrific Battle at Antietam three days later.

Just over forty years old, and after hectic years in Washington and New York, GATH envisioned this as the site of refuge, a place where he could regroup, recharge and enjoy the country life. And so he began a new phase of his life, fueled by a new passion and funded by the old one: writing.

Near the still-rural town of Boonsboro, Maryland, and just a mile from the tiny hamlet of Burkittsville (now famous for the being the site of filming for *The Blair Witch Project*, a 1990s independent movie) the area today is remarkably unchanged by the passing of 130 years.

W.R. Hamilton describes the setting in a later article that appeared in the *Baltimore Sun*:

> *Dividing Frederick and Washington counties in Maryland is the ridge of the easternmost range of the Appalachians, known for a few miles north of the Potomac River as the South Mountains. Here it is flanked by the famous Middletown Valley, hedged in by the Catoctin spur on the one side and by a little vale called Pleasant Valley, hedged in by another mountain spur, Maryland Heights of "Ossawatomie" John Brown fame, on the other. This is a region of numerous gaps, two of which—Crampton's and Turner's—in the South Mountains, were carried after a series of sharp engagements by the Union forces under McClellan on September 14, 1862, making inevitable the general conflict between McClellan and Lee on Antietam battlefield three days later.*
>
> *The lower gap is Crampton's, and on the summit along both sides of the road that passes through it is Gapland, the site selected by George Alfred Townsend, who obtained fame in the Civil War times under the pseudonym of GATH.*

In the article, GATH tells Hamilton his story of why he chose this site:

> *About twenty-two years ago, when I was at work on Katy of Catoctin, I found that I had been all over the ground where the scenes of that novel are laid, with the exception of Crampton's Gap, and determined to drive there one day from Harpers Ferry, which I did. I was making a sketch on the spot where the war correspondent's arch now stands and was accosted there by*

a Dunkard preacher, who manifested curiosity concerning a proceeding so strange to the mountain-top, then uninhabited.

I learned from him the owner of the mountain land. The design I then cherished was the writing of a series of American novels similar to the Waverly series. The proximity of the spot to the railroad on one side of the mountain and to a village on the other side, the magnificent views which it commands, and the general picturesque of the scenery inspired me with the idea that it was the ideal location, not far from Washington, where I had my winter home.

I started negotiations the next day, bought it and added other strips. I first built a frame dwelling, now called Askelon, but, learning that surface stone was cheap and available, I soon afterward began the erection of the Hall and the Lodge. Additions were made from time to time until the property is now five residences and some twenty structures. My wife lived here until her death, or from 1886 to 1903. A reason for seeking a country place was the difficulty of finding room in a city house for my collections, and the desire for retirement.

By 1886, GATH had built his country retreat and was spending more and more time there. For the *Cincinnati Enquirer,* he describes the need for refuge and the process of discovery and settling in:

Before the season of watering-place letters is over, I see an opportunity to describe a country place, and amend some well-meant sketches of Gapland, where I nominally live. Having communicated with your readers almost daily since May of 1876, a sketch to them of the surroundings of a frequent correspondent will not be deemed exploitation.

The necessity of some place of retirement for even two or three days, while pursuing an extensive correspondence for the press, with incidental student life and some attempts at literature became apparent to me from the time I commenced to publish, thirty-five years ago.

Intercourse with men and vigorous conversation have always been as exhausting of my temperament and mentality as writing. I gave up lecturing, as I was never let alone when I had something to deliver, or had to spend the whole day at hard work, describing myself or hearing others describe their investments, before I started to fulfill my contract. Man is always interesting, but he is also fatiguing. Love itself becomes surfeited.

I made a small investment in the spot selected, and concluded to put up there a kind of hunter's lodge, with a stall for two horses and a stall for a cow, a place for a buggy and a living room. Before I made this design complete, I found that masonry was not costly, and I added to my lodge two stone buildings, one for servants and the second for indoor recreation, with dormitories above. Instead of going as formerly to various places for recuperation, I now went to this place, and it was more than a year before my family saw it, they meantime of the opinion that I had become notional and meant to be a hermit.

To this place I added a little from time to time, members of my family making suggestions, and after four or five years of summer residence there, the family concluded that they had rather spend eight months in the country than divide the year between the country and the city. That settled the matter of the city house. I was a countryman, but with my foot loose to go anywhere I chose. Hereafter I could make my vacations and adventures to the city from the country, instead of to the country from the city. The winter was left open to me when the cities were full of people and amusements and themes to go thither, and instead of long terms when the city house was shut up, I could always find my family in a cool situation, 1,000 feet above the sea area and 300 feet above the surrounding valleys, with their gardens, small orchards, flower-beds, milk, chickens, etc., not only at hand, but ever developing.

Every aspect of the project, from the design and function of the buildings to the materials used, the furnishings and even the decorative elements, was chosen by GATH. He enjoyed the creative process, as it called on talents not expressed by writing.

To place the location for the reader, he points out that:

the battlefield at Antietam is six or seven miles from me. The National Road is in sight of my house, which connected the Tide-water country with Cumberland and Wheeling. The general basis of population is old German, with intrusions of Virginians, Scotch-Irish and Tide-water English. A railroad, built since the war, runs from Potomac to Hagerstown, which is a general railroad center, and passes within a mile of my residence. Fourteen miles east of me is old Frederick City, a place much older than Baltimore. Eighteen miles to the northwest is Hagerstown.

It was this railroad, a spur of the B&O, which made the location ideal for GATH. By his calculations, he could be in Washington in ninety minutes; he could breakfast at his country home, take the train to Washington, lunch with colleagues, attend meetings and still be at home in the country in time for dinner. Surprisingly, it still takes about ninety minutes to make that trip, in spite of interstates and our fast-moving cars. Today's traveler sits trapped in traffic back-ups, able to listen to his car radio for diversion, with little else to ease the frustration. GATH sat in a comfortable railroad car, perhaps smoking a cigar, talking with other travelers and able to make good use of his time by writing or reading. He continues in the *Cincinnati Enquirer:*

> *The first year or two I was at Gapland, I built 2,000 to 3,000 feet of stone wall, picked the ground in the gap clear of rocks, and commenced lawns and patches for cultivation. By the next spring I had three houses, as has been mentioned, and each of these has been extended in successive years.*

What started as a summer home quickly became a summer estate. The first building that he had used as a residence became a barn. Next to it was the first house, which he called Askelon. (Both Gath and Askelon are ancient cities in Israel.)

When reading the descriptions of the buildings, it is obvious that GATH must have had help with building all this, but few names are mentioned. Certainly, Bessie was a partner, as she was often at home while he traveled, which is why the archives hold such an extensive collection of personal correspondence, as well as his published newspaper work.

The earliest buildings at Gapland: the barn, outbuildings and Askelon. The arch was the last structure built on the estate.

Visitors to the museum at Gathland, when seeing the extensive and elaborate estate he built, often assume he had family money, as no mere reporter could have earned that much. The answer to that is that he was no mere reporter but a well-paid journalist whose prodigious output paid for his building ventures.

Still, he was not a Rockefeller or a Vanderbilt, backed by inherited family money, and he was inclined to spend money rather too freely on his favorite projects.

The letters to Bessie and his children provide great insight into not only his activities but his personality and lifestyle as well. Mention of finances appear often—money was always a concern—as he writes from Liverpool in 1880:

> *It is dear, dear living here, though on the surface it looks cheap. My breakfast this morning was two shillings (half a dollar) for only toast, butter, coffee and some kind of jam.*

From the steamer *Brighton*, crossing from New Haven to Dieppe in 1880, he wrote:

> *I gave $30 in Lisbon for a full wool suit of blue Melton cloth and heavy mixed pants. An overcoat will cost $25. Since I left home, I have spent $100 and made $200 as I compute.*

From Chicago in 1884:

> *I ought to be ashamed for having overlooked sending you some money. I have been dreadfully busy. Enclosed is a cheque for $30...I would very much like to go this summer to the Blue Ridge Mountains at Pennmar in Western Maryland to write my novel. Would you like to go there? It is a new hotel about 1,500 ft above the valley and only about 3 hours from Baltimore.*

The letters (notes, most of them) also indicate that Bessie must have served as building supervisor and general "clerk of the works" in his absence, giving her very specific instructions to be passed along to a man named Albaugh (apparently a contractor and overseer), as well as sending checks with amounts to be paid the workmen. Here are two excerpts from his letters regarding Bessie's part in the building of Gapland, both dated 1888:

Dear Bessie,

You might tell Albaugh to see the plasterer and find what he is going to plaster the upstairs three rooms for in hard finish, for which the plaster of Paris and white sand are already on the spot. He has charged 7 or 8 cents a square yard generally for common plastering. I have got a stained glass transom 18¼ inches high and 26¼ inches wide. Ask Albaugh if it will go in or over the front door or the south window; and what size sash required to make of it.

Affectionately,
Alfred

You must write me to New York what changes have been made in the style of that billiard hall, and their measurements so that I can see what to get for the building. I have got Baker here and am dictating three letters a day. I enclose check for $30 for 2,000 bricks. Pay cash for them and use the best.

By the time the family moved back from New York in 1889, Gapland Hall was quite habitable, and other buildings would soon be finished According to a local paper, the Townsends entertained. They certainly had a splendid residence, which was built for great entertaining.

Gapland Hall, looking up from the road that divides the barn, the outbuildings and Askelon from the larger homes on the hill.

Fine craftsmanship and careful design characterize the buildings on Townsend's estate. This is a view of the Den and Library.

Another view of the Den and Library, the largest building on the estate.

The ladies gather at Gapland. If the trees and vegetation are to be believed, it is summer. They seem very formally dressed for a summer event in the country.

A small gathering of guests at Gapland.

The *Valley Register* reports that "about 100 persons from Frederick and Washington counties attended the dance given at the residence of Mr. George Alfred Townsend at Gapland last Friday night." If they entertained 100 persons from the two neighboring counties, it would seem that they had made friends locally. The stories about that later reported the entertaining of "the cream of Washington and Baltimore society" were exaggerated, although they did continue to entertain friends and associates from those two cities.

In addition to Gapland Hall and the Den and Library, the largest buildings, there were the earliest house, Askelon, the Lodge and several cottages. The cottages were used for family members or rented out to others. With upward of fifteen bedrooms available in the family homes, it would seem that there was room for family without putting them in separate buildings, but GATH must have had his reasons.

6

BUILDING THE ESTATE BEGINS...
AND CONTINUES

*G*ATH certainly must have been a surprise to the local folk, the farmers and tradesmen who lived in that part of Western Maryland. Palatial estates were few and far between, and even people of wealth in Western Maryland were not acquainted with the unusual architecture styles he favored.

In Hindes's work on Gath, she continues to present him as modest and unassuming, even after he built his estate. Photos and descriptions in newspaper articles show that it is large and very different from its neighbors in this rural and somewhat rustic setting. Hindes notes that

> *writers have tried to make him appear eccentric. The fact that he loved nature and art is an adequate reason. As other men collect stamps, paintings and various articles, so Townsend designed and built houses. With him it was a hobby. The idea of building for ostentations never once occurred to him; he would have hated the idea.*

Certainly, GATH designed his houses to please himself and, like most of us, wanted to live in comfort, surrounded by beautiful things. But it is also true that the words "ostentatious," "flamboyant" and "pretentious" were used then and now to accurately describe him and his estate. His buildings were an expression of his larger-than-life personality, his artistic ability and his financial success; for someone raised in such impecunious circumstances, it was surely his dream come true.

Later newspaper accounts rhapsodized about lavish parties, French chefs and fine art and boasted that guests were the cream of Washington society. In his professional life, and sometimes socially, he was acquainted with the rich, famous and talented. Still, the Townsends were worlds away from the Rockefellers and the Vanderbilts and even the most distant hangers-on of those social circles.

His own descriptions of his buildings are matter-of-fact and practical.

> *Through my lawn runs a public road, on the top of the mountain. On the north side of the road is a stone barn with a spire, having fourteen stalls for animals, seven on each side; the size of the barn is forty-six feet by thirty feet; the stone walls are two feet thick, and terra cotta horse-heads and inscription dates are set in the stone work. Near this is a carriage house and harness room in the front and a living room for the overseer. What was formerly a stable has been transformed into a seven-roomed house for servants on the same side of the road, and is called "Askelon."*

Apparently the carriage house is the "kind of hunter's lodge" he refers to earlier, in which he lived while starting the larger buildings. The transformation to Askelon, a house, must have been made when the barn was built to house the animals and equipment. Ever practical, GATH notes that the barn has a balcony along the front, which affords a fine view of the valleys, and has windows in the corners so that it might eventually be made into a house if needed. The remains of the barn can still be seen at Gathland State Park and show the visitor just what it takes to make a masonry wall three feet thick. There was also a windmill near the "working" part of the estate.

GATH was very much the artist, and although the details of each building were designed for functionality, ornamentation was not overlooked: "I have built no houses without adding some ornament to them. Even the woodhouse, which is made of stone, is skylighted above and has wing walls with pedestals for vases and flowers."

He named the estate Gapland, "in order not to give it personality," but of course, it quickly developed its own personality, one rather similar to GATH's own: grandiose, unique and somewhat flamboyant.

On the opposite side of the road that bisected his lawn and on a hillside (the barn, Askelon and utility buildings were on a flat, meadow-like area), he situated Gapland Hall, the family residence, which was completed in 1885, and the Den and Library just a little later. Other buildings came later but were hardly mentioned in his writings.

One of many rooms in Gapland Hall. It was fully furnished and decorated in the somewhat overworked style of the Victorian era.

If other men collected stamps or art as a hobby, GATH collected everything. His collections of antiques, sculpture, paintings, memorabilia, souvenirs from his travels and decorative items furnished his homes. He remarked in a letter to a friend that he has several buildings, and "none is without embellishment." Probably the most prized possession among his many collections was his library. He was a voracious reader and used his books for reference to inform his writing and lecturing. He explains how he acquired it and how it was used:

> *I commenced to buy articles of instruction and embellishment very early, and have gradually filled in the outlines of my library, until it is probably more effective than any newspaper library in this country. It may be said to commence with aids to expression, such as books on philology, foreign dictionaries, concordances—whatever, being upon the spot aids the memory without looking at it, as is often the case with a book. Next, books of fact in different departments—the sciences, natural history, natural philosophy, physics, books of the trades from different periods. Here is a book for instance*

on how they distilled whiskey before it was done by steam. Here is a book on navigation; so that if I ever chose to describe how Columbus crossed the ocean I could almost run his ship. Here is a history of lawyers. Here are Blackstone and Kent and military books and books on fortifications.

He goes on to list other categories, all carefully collected to serve his purpose—histories of every nation, maps and atlases of different periods of the country, gazetteers showing the transformation of the land, how the roads ran at a certain time, all the American cities of note, the local histories, the state papers and correspondence of American political leaders such as Washington, Hamilton, Jefferson, Calhoun, Webster, John Adams, John Quincy Adams, etc.

These books were not collected merely for display, to impress the visitor, but carefully selected to give him a well-rounded reference library. He had high praise for "men who have, at very little profit, I fear, kept together in consultable form the archives of their country."

He bemoans the decline of high thought:

When a novel which has taken a person years to write, such as Daniel Deronda, *appears at fifteen or twenty cents. I have very little respect for people who will pay five cents to shine their boots and not five cents to shine their heads, who grudge five cents for a newspaper and give five cents for a glass of beer.*

In that same line of thought, he comments on another common practice that denigrates the creation of a library: "It is surprising to see how the females in the house will shut up a big parlor every day in the year but a dozen or so and grudge the use of its wall-room to a man with a library." The library eventually held over five thousand books.

Clearly, the Den and Library was the storehouse of his ambitions and accomplishments, his collected knowledge and his greatest treasure. It was for him the heart of a refined and elegant existence, a tradition that has recently been revived, a space that in the twenty-first century we now refer to as a "man cave," a very big and very well-appointed one indeed.

The same attention to detail that characterized his writing informs the reader of how the Den and Library was designed and furnished:

If you will drop by my library you will see a room with a wooden ceiling and a great fire-place, which will hold a log seven feet long;

above it caryatides in terra cotta, to the ceiling sustain a mirror. One
of John Brown's pikes, used at Harpers Ferry, is over the fire-place.

He went on to mention paintings of Edward Gibbon, Aaron Burr, Schiller
and Scott, Andrew Jackson and other impressive historical figures. And
befitting a man of his means, there is a billiards table. In one alcove is a
stained-glass panel with a giant's head run through by a quill, and the
inscription "Tell it not in Gath."

This den connects with my bedroom and the bedroom with the bath by very
narrow doors, as I can see no reason for making a room all door. Most of
the pictures in the bedroom are illustrative of Henrietta Maria, the queen
of Charles I, for whom the State of Maryland was named, though I find
that fact to be rather obscure in Maryland.

Every painting or sculpture or decorative element was chosen to make a
pleasing and cohesive presentation. The variety in his selections indicated the vast

Townsend in his Den and Library, probably in the study. Every room in that building and in
Gapland Hall was filled with splendid furnishings, art and objects collected in his travels.

scope of his interests in history and its players. One room displayed the homes of various naturalists and workers, from Pliny and Benjamin West to Rubens, Walter Scott and Dickens. Also among his collections were specific references to his part in now-historic events, such as the piece of scaffold from the John Brown hanging and a stone from the foundation of Alexander Hamilton's house.

W.R. Hamilton contributes impressions formed from a visit to the estate in 1907 for an article in the *Baltimore Sun*. GATH was sixty-seven years old, and his most vigorous years were behind him. His wife had died, his physical health and his finances had deteriorated and he was alone in his beloved Gapland. The following passage is in response to a question put to him by W.R Hamilton:

> *Lonely and isolated? Do not three mails pass by each day? Are not towns and crowds of easy access when desired? Can he not, by simply passing from room to room, enjoy the company of the world's greatest men, whose good does live after them is not interred with their bones? No more is the Hall enlivened by throngs of guests, happy in the acquaintance of so entertaining a host, for Mrs. Townsend is not there to share the pleasant duties of hospitality and permit the diligent scribe to have some time for labors, and there is none to take her place.*

Hamilton summarizes the sumptuous surroundings at Gapland:

> *Several commodious residences, a large barn, numerous small buildings pavilions, fine orchards, an oil storage plant and a cemetery are all within the limits of Gapland's hundred acres.*
>
> *Strange place, it may be, to find one of the finest private libraries in the land, pictures so numerous that the owner has not counted them, costly marbles, bronzes, pottery and other adornments fit for palatial mansions, but Mr. Townsend has here 5,000 of his 8,000 selected volumes; pictures crowd the wall of 34 rooms and many hallways and there are other works of art in bewildering profusion. Here Mr. Townsend chose to establish a retreat 22 years ago in order to pursue his literary vocation. He has embellished it with treasures from all parts of the world.*

Hamilton seemed both fascinated and possibly even awestruck by the things he saw: brick fireplaces decorated with tiles from different countries; a grandfather's clock from Barrett's Chapel in Dover, Delaware; handsome pieces of antique rosewood furniture; family pictures; and other works of art and pictures of every description, including a splendid three-quarter-length portrait of the author.

Hamilton also mentioned the stained-glass window in the den, which he said is the coat of arms of the Marquis of Townshend, who has ancestry in common with that of the author. It contains a Latin motto, which he was told was (very freely) translated as "Ennobled for our fidelity.' This raises some doubt, as Townsend was said to have made an effort to trace his family tree, apparently with little success, as he later remarked that "it is foolish to try to make a family tree out of so much dead wood."

For clarity, it should be noted once again that the Den and Library and Gapland Hall are two separate buildings. Most references claim there were about fifty rooms when counting all the residences at Gapland. The Den and Library, used by GATH as a residence and sanctuary, contained twenty rooms; Gapland Hall, presided over by Mrs. Townsend, about fourteen; and the Lodge, a much smaller stone building with a frame kitchen attached to it, was used for dining informally and to house a few servants on the second floor. Although both of the larger houses had dining rooms, in summer the family took their meals there.

The Lodge still stands at Gathland and is one of the two museums, this one devoted to the Civil War battle that occurred there at Crampton's Gap. Although Askelon and the Den and Library are gone, and the majority of Gapland Hall as well, several of the stone cottages he had built for rental and the tollhouse for the turnpike still stand and are privately owned.

Gapland Hall, the family residence, is not described with as much detail as the Den and Library, but it was a large and handsome Victorian Gothic–style stone building. GATH describes it as "the most extensive on the place, about 100 feet long and a portion of it sixty feet wide."

It, too, in the Victorian style of the time, was stuffed with fine furniture and fabrics, art treasures and bric-a-brac—the best that money and a good eye for quality could obtain. No catalogues of the furnishings are available, but a piece of hand-painted china, purchased in France, tastefully bearing the word "Gapland" in gold letters, gives credence to stories of the extent to which he went in making his "retreat" opulent. When a great-great granddaughter visited the Gathland museum dedicated to GATH and the War Correspondent's Arch, she exclaimed, "That's my china! I have a service for twelve. My mother still has the other thirty-eight place settings!" Later, a great-great grandson visited and quietly mentioned that he, too, has a service for twelve. That brings the count to more than fifty place settings, and there could be more. And if there was enough china to serve fifty or more, they would have had an equal number of settings of silver, glassware and other accoutrements.

A piece of the hand-painted china created for Gapland in France. *Photo by author.*

A fondness for furnishings did not limit GATH's involvement in less glamorous aspects of making a comfortable home. He reports that:

> *the water supply comes from a well, obtaining water at fifty-four feet, to the wonder of the mountaineers, who had never tried, and from a tank holding one hundred-fifty barrels, which is entirely filled in the spring of the year by a small rain at the spring, in a ravine one thousand one hundred feet distant and more than 200 feet lower than the tank. This brave little heart works whenever there is water in the spring, and as we use the full tank, a supply is ever running in of water without any trace of lime or hard matter. I have besides a cistern to take the water from the Den and Library, which holds about one hundred thirty barrels.*
>
> *Piping the water around this place was the most trying task upon the pocket nerves, but nothing pays like it; to have running water on every floor in the country and bathrooms enough is the luxury of all ages.*

He also winterized the Den and Library:

> *So that if I choose at any time to come here in the winter through ennui or with a task in hand, I can live in a stone house heated by a powerful furnace with flues, hot and cold water, partitions weather-lined, open fireplaces and a series of studies opening into other rooms from the main library. This general house is called the den. Its main floor consists of a library 49 by 24 feet, a study shaped like an L in two rooms, a sanctum and writing room, a bedroom and bath. Over this floor are ten bedrooms. Beneath the den, on the slope of the mountain, are injected domestic apartments, a refectory, kitchen, dining room and smoking room.*

How is it possible that these wonderful places disintegrated into oblivion?

7

Gapland Flourishes, and the Family Grows Older

By the time GATH had settled in with his family at Gapland, in about 1885, he seems to have overcome whatever youthful shyness he claimed to possess and had became a compelling personality. In his newspaper work, and with his novels and poetry, he was confident and sure of his place in the cosmos. He was also known to speak his mind rather forcefully, earning him a reputation as somewhat imperious. Perhaps because of this perceived arrogance, some critics were inclined to harsh reviews of his writing, especially his poetry.

Construction was still going on after Gapland Hall, the Lodge and the Den and Library had been completed. The *Valley Register* reports in May 1893 that "George Alfred Townsend has completed a pretty Queen Anne–style cottage on his place at Gapland. The cottage has been rented to a friend for the summer." It also relates that "the stonework on the Gapland pike toll-house is about finished and the carpenters have taken charge. The building constructed entirely of stone is very substantial. It is located about fifty yards from the summit."

The tollhouse was part of the Gapland Turnpike Company's newly built toll road. Townsend was secretary of the company, which was made up of several local businessmen. All was not well with the toll road, however, according to an 1893 edition of the *Valley Register*. Local farmers and tradesmen did not like the idea of paying to have access to the railroad in Gapland, even though the road had been improved.

Ever since the organization of the Gapland Turnpike Company, there has been a visible current of dissatisfaction existing among the people of this vicinity. It has been largely among those people who contributed money and labor toward piking the lane to the station before the pike was organized. When the pike was organized, these persons were asked to make up the difference between the amount they had given to the road, and the par value of a share of stock. This many declined to do, as they were opposed to the pike. So the matter stood until the opening of the pike. Just now the opposition is organizing and a plan is being agitated to open a new road from the top of the mountain to Gapland station. The route is to go down the Rohrersville road several hundred yards, thence across the intervening farms by way of old stone church to the station, which would make a road of about the same length and easier grades than the old road. The right of way has been secured over nearly all of the proposed route, but no definite action taken. The pike people, on the other hand, claim to be able to block the movement, even if they have to move the gate at the top of the mountain. Whatever may be done is likely to cause trouble. It is to be regretted that any disagreement should have arisen over the enterprise, which is such a decided improvement over the old road.

Although Townsend was only part of a group of local businessmen who formed the corporation to build a toll road, the venture aroused strong opposition among some of the local farmers who used the road to get their commodities to the Gapland train station for shipping. The road went through Townsend's property and provided direct access to the station, which might have seemed to the local farmers more advantageous to GATH than to themselves. They solved their problem by going south to the Weaverton station, which was a bit farther but free.

After GATH's estate was abandoned, some locals were said to have contributed to the vandalism that helped push the buildings more quickly into disrepair by appropriating some of the beautiful building materials from his structures for their own homes, apparently believing "he owed them" for charging them to use a road they had always used. Builders of new homes were also suspected of helping themselves, particularly to the fine ornamental features he incorporated into every building.

His reputation among his Western Maryland neighbors comes down to us through a few who claimed to have known him. His buildings, his personality and his style of living were foreign to them. He made few friends among them, but that is not an unusual relationship between longtime residents of a community and new, sometimes seasonal, arrivals of a different social and financial background.

GATH had always maintained a residence in Washington, D.C., but after the buildings were complete, the family spent more and more time at Gapland. As a public figure, a well-known writer, he has been written about extensively; his personal life is less well known.

He moved around a good bit in Washington before moving to New York. From 1869 to 1875, he is listed in the census at 319 B Street North, 916 17th Street NW and 1020 17th Street NW. After the building of Gapland, from 1894 to 1914, the time of his death, his Washington home was at 229 1st Street NE.

Just ninety minutes by train, GATH commuted to Washington and other cities when necessary, but he and his family were able to live the greater part of the year at Gapland.

It is known that he traveled widely and enjoyed the society of political figures, other writers and the cognoscenti of his era. Not as much is known about his personal life. Fortunately, this very important aspect of the multitalented GATH is illustrated by the gift of his personal correspondence of his great-granddaughter Dorothy Rasmussen. Mrs. Rasmussen has been the keeper of the flame and has shared with the Gathland State Park and the museum there information that brings to life the man who lived at Gapland and his family.

By 1885, most of Gapland was in working order. At the time of the transition to their summer home, Genevieve was eighteen years old, and George Alfred Jr. was eleven. GATH later acknowledged in a letter to Genevieve, "You never were a country girl," which was true. Most of her life was spent in their homes in Washington and New York. And if Bessie missed city life, she surely had enough to do at Gapland, managing the construction, the household and the children, as well as entertaining.

Little mention is made of George Alfred Jr. during his years at Gapland, and he seems to have vanished from history as an adult. Records show that he married Ila Rogers, and they had a son, Roger Gath, who married Anne Mead in 1932. The line continued with George Alfred Townsend III and Roger Gath Townsend Jr. and then George Alfred Townsend IV, Roger Gath Townsend III and Richard Mead Townsend (see Appendix C). Still, it seems no one has anything to add to the legacy of George Alfred Townsend Jr.

GATH's comments in an excerpt from an undated letter to his daughter, Genevieve, illuminate the tensions in his relationship with his son:

George Alfred Jr. and Genevieve Townsend as children.

Left: George Alfred Townsend Jr. and his wife, Ila, with their son, Roger Gath Townsend.

Right: George Alfred Townsend Jr.

Alfred T. has a woman on the brain and writes letters all day and schemes and dreams and I know not what to think. He sent six great barrels to the house to pack up things and I suppose take them off. I found them coming in and asked what they were for. He was excited like a crazy person which I believe him to be, talked about his "rights" and threatened; so that I have said only necessary things to him for three days.

In my opinion, an insane impulse started him to plunder the house. This while his mother was hardly conscious. He is clear out of Cash Register and the President does not see him. Every time he gets a job, he gets a woman, madly matrimonial and yet it is dubious whether he is fit to marry.

He combines the child and the brute, breaks out in a perfectly causeless outrage without other occasion than a mad brain, and I am in despair of him and heartily wished I might go into the grave with your mother when she is so ill. He is now ashamed and sulks. What is mine would be his. Why does he sack the house? To find presents to a woman again and take them back. He does not go to the library (Congress). He talks about becoming the general agent for a safety razor.

Although this letter is not dated, the mention of Bessie's imminent death places the time sometime during her long illness, probably between 1901 and 1903. George Alfred Jr. would have been about twenty-eight years old. There were other issues with him, including an episode in which he convinced his ailing mother to give him the deed to one of the stone cottages GATH had built on the estate. GATH reveals in a letter that he hired an attorney, who succeeded in reclaiming the property.

It is not clear what kind of parent GATH was; though he was surely absent a lot, he seemed to have a continuing and congenial relationship with his daughter. Genevieve had five children, four of whom survived into old age. She visited Gapland with her children, and later the children, especially George Alfred (GATH's grandson), with whom he was quite close, visited for longer periods.

The latest reference to George Alfred Jr. comes in a letter in 1903 to Genevieve: "My Alfred has not written me for eleven days. I suppose he is in matrimony again and desperate for salary. He says he spent $80 for [illegible] and his automobile is his last toy. The despair of confidence in this son is a heavy grief; he is so unforeseeing and repetitive in his follies."

Genevieve married Edmund Bonaventure, a man just three years younger than her father. Bonaventure was a widower, with adult children of his own, and a friend of her father. He was French and had become wealthy as an inventor; he also was a dealer in books. They lived in Manhattan and visited family in his native France. Genevieve and Bonaventure had five children: George Alfred Bonaventure, Genevieve, Yvonne, Simone and Bessie, who was born and died in 1886. Bonaventure died just three years after GATH, leaving Genevieve a widow for thirty four years.

Bonaventure was a good husband and a good son-in-law. He published some of GATH's writing and helped assemble his carefully chosen library, then helped in disposing of it when that became necessary.

Jerry Shields, in his book *Gath's Literary Work and Folk*, suggests that GATH and Bessie did not have a good marriage: "Theirs had not been a very close marriage even in the early years, as his writings and travels left him little time for family life. Even at Gapland, where he had finally begun to settle down, he and Bessie lived mostly apart in the separate houses he had built to protect his privacy."

It was very much the style at the time for men of means to have separate dwellings. Today, the custom has resurfaced; men have "their own space" and currently call it a "man cave." Bessie lived at Gapland Hall, GATH in

Genevieve Townsend as a young woman.

Left: Genevieve Townsend Bonaventure as a married woman. Her husband was just three years younger than her father, and she lived as a widow for twenty-four years.

Right: Edmund F. Bonaventure, husband of Genevieve Townsend and Townsend's friend and son-in-law.

his Den and Library and relatives, grandchildren and their nannies lived in Askelon when they visited.

The years of correspondence between them suggest that they were close in many ways, if not in physical proximity at all times. She certainly was a partner in the marriage and kept the home fires burning. Their marriage was no less solid than those of women who are married to sea captains, military officers and others whose work takes them away from home for long periods.

For his part, GATH's letters express love and fidelity often and in glowing terms. In the first year of the marriage, he writes, "I wish the work of life was a love letter that I might spend it all in conveying to you the assurance of my deep and constant affection for you. Now you are sick and need my presence, but do you never feel me beside you? If not beloved, there is no truth in apparitions; for I am always dreaming and thinking of your dear face...We must be help, comfort, sympathy and ambition to one another."

There were many declarations of love throughout the years, often imploring Bessie not to worry about his fidelity, to be patient, to understand his hopes for their future together. He also writes of the tribulations of constant travel, the loneliness, bad food, illness and boredom. And he writes of the pleasant interludes, occasionally mentioning the scenery and the "lovely girls of the region."

Probably in response to a letter of complaint from Bessie, in 1867 he writes:

> *As soon as I got here, I went to the Post Office to ask for letters. There were two, both from you, and I read them very anxiously. I am sorry to hear that you were unwell; you must keep up your spirits and remember that my absence is our very bread and happiness. You lack a patient spirit, Bessie. Do something to amuse yourself. Knit an afghan or something. I want a fine robe for traveling very badly.*
>
> *I tell you frankly that I will not come home till I am done. I am absent from you very little; and heretofore you have always traveled with me. Employ your mind. Do something. Knit a chair-back! Study French! Make more of your life than mere pining and gayety. I love you constantly and rationally. Take good care of the little one; soon she will begin to perceive and reason; and if she sees you with no object in life, her own life will grow purposeless. Feel and know that I always love you.*

As the years passed, the letters are perhaps less passionate and romantic, but they continue to offer a window into their relationship, as well as a kind of diary of people and everyday events that would have seemed too trivial to put in memoirs of historical import.

Fraught with peril when analyzing the relationships of others is the forming of conclusions about relationships from a distance, particularly within the very different climate of Victorian manners. Many fashionable Victorians patterned their lives after the British aristocracy, with residences larger than they needed, nannies and governesses to distance the children from the parents and servants to wait on them—if they could afford it. GATH was nouveau riche, but he knew what old money looked like and determined to live like it.

Another thought on the marriage: Though Bessie might have fretted early in the marriage about his absence, they seem to have created a good working partnership over the years and together blended parenting with his career and her homemaking to create a good life for everyone, except perhaps George Alfred Jr.

And finally, I offer this conjecture: Men like GATH—talented, intelligent, ambitious, acquisitive, intensely inquisitive and highly energetic—can also be overwhelming, difficult and even exhausting for the average person. They are interesting, charming and delightful, but a little bit goes a long way. It is possible that Bessie's life was quite full with her own pursuits and responsibilities, and as she grew more confident in her role in his life, she welcomed the quiet that came in his absence and could welcome him home more enthusiastically because of it.

Gapland could not have been so carefully constructed without Bessie's participation. This note sent in 1888 is typical of her part in it:

Dear Bessie,

In a few days the boxes of books will arrive and three boxes of crockery, etc. I very much fear the china will be broken. Do not open the books.

I shall put the books in the big room of the new library building...and take away the furniture against the wall, sending down the shelves here to be used and have glass doors made to protect the books. That is the object of that building and there they will be secure. Have all the library book boxes put on the main library floor and take up the best rug there. I have a bad cold from having got wet in the severe rain of the last five days.

How would you like your room painted in calcimined terra cotta and hung with paintings? I sent you much of my stain for mantels.

Affectionately,
Alfred

And Bessie wrote in 1879:

Dear Alf,

Your suit came yesterday and they sent it on to you from downstairs. The money came from the Graphic. *I will send the watch today fr. Genevieve. I gave the stenographer 5.00 to go to Phila. with. Mr. Schaffer called here a few minutes to see you, something about "Bull Domingo." Mr. Thompson was here yesterday. To the visitors, I suppose you will be home on Saturday. We miss you very much. The children are well.*

Poor Mrs. Fish is thought to be dying. The 21ˢᵗ of this month we will have been married 14 years and as much in love as the first day we married, can you say the same. Then on the 23ʳᵈ of the month is the day our little darling Donn was born—he would have been nine years had he lived, he was too noble and good for this world, highly sensitive and so lovable—he was my idol. This boy Alfred is quicker, but has too much old Adam in him. Genevieve reads and walks out. Everyone is delighted she is going to private school. Write when you have time.

Yours Lovingly,
Bessie

GATH, too, continues to use endearing terms when writing to Bessie, this in a letter from London in July 1880:

Dear Bessie,

You are the principal companion of my days, even when so far absent. I said to myself tonight: "Stop this thinking about your wife so much, or you will be wretched to go home too soon."

He tells her that he spent the day between the Tower of London and Windsor Castle, which he says is "an ancient castle in great part rebuilt, but all is the same style of the middle ages, with great towers and battlements, the whole standing on a lofty hill over the winding Thames. The Queen's jewels we saw today, with the official scepters, crowns, maces and other shining trash, cost $17,500,000, or four millions more than the Capitol of the United States." No wonder he came back to America ready to build a castle of his own.

Then comes the usual financial accounting: "I paid for two silk hdks., two pairs best quality Alexandre's gloves, a pair of suspenders of hideskin(?) made to order, and three silk bows, the sum of 11s and some pence, or about $2.75, the price of 1 pair of kids at home. The gloves were made for A.T. Stewart and bore his imprint; they were 87 cents a pair. Immense silk handkerchiefs here cost only 75 cts."

Not all of his letters were travelogues, however; some complained of illness, the cold, the heat, the food or whatever unpleasantness he encountered. Still, Bessie must have occasionally felt little frissons of envy when she read of his meeting some of the world's most interesting people—such as the Prince of Wales and his bride, the Empress of Russia, famous entertainers, presidents—or of the closing scenes of the war between Prussia and Austria.

Not many remain, but Bessie wrote notes, to GATH and to her daughter, Genevieve. Usually these were cheerful and breezy but a bit wistful. She was

Townsend, looking much like a sedate banker, circa 1906.

very close to her grandchildren, and they wrote and visited. Genevieve's only son, George Alfred Bonaventure, is referred to by Bessie and GATH as "your Alfred," to distinguish him from his uncle, Alfred Jr., or sometimes they were called G.B. and A.T. GATH referred to his own son, Alfred Jr., as "my Alfred" when writing to his daughter, Genevieve, who also had an Alfred.

The lengthy 1881 article in *Lippincott's* "An Interviewer Interviewed" begins with this description of GATH's physical attributes: "Mr. George Alfred Townsend is a large man, weighing two hundred and twenty pounds in his clothes, about five feet ten inches in height, with a smooth, sanguine complexion, high cheek-bones, and broad face, and the general appearance of a portly man of business with neither the natural nor the affected signs of his vocation."

It is almost certain that GATH is both the interviewer and the subject of the interview in this article. One-sentence questions are followed by long, detailed answers, and the questions seem designed to move the narrative chronologically through his life story as he wished to have it told.

James Rankin Young, one of GATH's friends, described him as:

> *a sociable man who liked to talk, but he talked about things and not about himself. He was a temperate man, but we often met at those old Washington saloons where there were chairs and tables, drank, smoked and talked; and Townsend was chief spokesman always and had a group about him. For a long time, he was the biggest earning correspondent in Washington.*

A friend of George Townsend Jr. who claimed to be a frequent guest at Gapland describes GATH as:

> *a big man, well over six feet, weighing about 300 pounds. And an unidentified writer said, "GATH is corpulent both in face and abdomen,*

and wears a fine specimen nose of the genus Wellington or Roman, has a low broad forehead, a big head, a large mouth and a double chin, and looks as if he knew what to do with a good dinner before letting it spoil...In his political writings, if there is anything for which he is particularly famous, it is the absolute accuracy of all his statements."

Later in his life, he was indeed "corpulent," as evidenced by the many photos that show him much changed from the dapper young man of the 1860s, when photographs show him as slender and stylishly attired. Though he did become corpulent, it is doubtful that he ever reached a height of "well over six feet." Probably five foot nine or ten inches is closer to the mark.

8

Their Lives at Gapland,

and the Beginning of the End

*U*nder the weight of Bessie's failing health and the increasing discomforts of his own, GATH soldiered on through the 1890s. He was still writing, still finding new topics of interest that justified his choice to make a career as an independent journalist. Whatever disappointments he might have experienced in not being widely accepted as a literary writer, he certainly achieved his goal of pursuing whatever interested him without an editor making choices for him, and he received many accolades in the process.

By this time, GATH was still active but slowing down. Critics and fans continued to comment on his work, and in May 1900, after the publication of a collection of his verses titled *Poems of Men and Events*, Montgomery Schuyler, a highly respected writer, cautiously praised him "not as a great American poet, but one worth reading." Jerry Shields, author of *GATH's Literary Work and Folk*, commented in his book, "He was not unaware of his shortcomings as a poet, but this had never stopped him from trying. He had failed to write the sort of poems which become immortal through inclusion in textbooks, but he had produced a number of verses able to stand in comparison with those individuals who had achieved reputations as poets. Of the huge amount of verse written during Victorian times, the vast majority was mediocre or worse."

Finances, always an issue for the Townsends, became increasingly problematic as his income diminished. At nearly sixty, he was no longer physically capable of maintaining the vigorous pace of earlier years, although his intellectual energy still propelled him toward writing. Further

Left: A bright green tin in which GATH cigars were sold, with the writer's motto: "The Pen Is Mightier than the Sword." *Photo by author.*

Below: Frey's Famous Cigar and Cigarette Factory produced cigars named after Townsend. It is not known whether he was paid for his endorsement or it was meant to honor a great journalist.

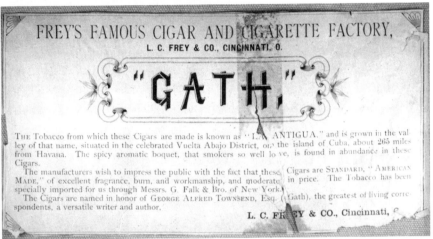

FREY'S FAMOUS CIGAR AND CIGARETTE FACTORY,
L. C. FREY & CO., CINCINNATI. O.

"GATH,"

THE Tobacco from which these Cigars are made is known as "LA ANTIGUA." and is grown in the valley of that name, situated in the celebrated Vuelta Abajo District, on the island of Cuba, about 265 miles from Havana. The spicy aromatic boquet, that smokers so well love, is found in abundance in these Cigars.

The manufacturers wish to impress the public with the fact that these Cigars are STANDARD, "AMERICAN MADE," of excellent fragrance, burn, and workmanship, and moderate in price. The Tobacco has been specially imported for us through Messrs. G. Falk & Bro. of New York.

The Cigars are named in honor of GEORGE ALFRED TOWNSEND, Esq. (Gath), the greatest of living correspondents, a versatile writer and author.

L. C. FREY & CO., Cincinnati, O.

complicating his situation was holding on to his lofty post in the literary firmament. Versatile as he was, younger people, new techniques and the general fading of his era eroded his best efforts. But he did not surrender.

One interesting opportunity that came to him along with fame was product endorsements. Several companies sought him out, one of them being the maker of pocketknives. The most well known was GATH cigars. Packaged in bright green tins and featuring the nib of a pen and the writer's inscription "The Pen Is Mightier than the Sword," they were no doubt the kind of cigars the manufacturer thought would appeal to smokers who were GATH's friends and associates. Another company also produced cigars with his endorsement.

Certain that the dynasty he created would go on forever, he built a mausoleum on the property, a fine stone building with a wrought-iron gate. A marble slab over the entrance read, "Good Night, Gath," and a J.W. Fiske metal dog sculpture, said to represent a dog he had been fond of, guarded the crypt from the roof. The Fiske catalogue identifies the dog as a French bloodhound, made of iron and zinc, and it could be purchased in metal finish or painted for about eighty dollars. A visitor to the museum recognized the statue as one called Morley's dog, which had survived the Johnstown flood in 1889 (the statue, not the dog) and is now the town's mascot.

One of the few edifices still standing, the mausoleum was never used—perhaps because his daughter told him at the time of Bessie's death that the property would not remain in the family or possibly because she felt it was too far for the Philadelphia-based family to travel to visit her mother's grave. Whatever the reason, both Bessie and GATH were buried in the family plot at Mount Laurel Cemetery in Philadelphia. The dog stayed at the Gathland site for a few years and then disappeared, ending up in a garage in Frederick. Heirs of the elderly owner of the dog at first promised it to the museum at Gathland, but when the property recently came to the heirs, one person insisted on keeping the dog. It was damaged and probably not worth much, but it would not be given to the museum at Gathland

Townsend purchased an ornamental iron and zinc statue sold by J.W. Fiske as a French bloodhound to sit atop his mausoleum. It disappeared from the property many years ago, and was found with a family living in Frederick. They declined to return it for display in the museum.

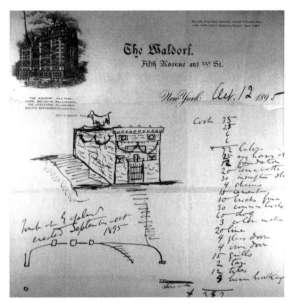

Left: This is the sketch for the mausoleum. Note the dog at the top and the marble slab over the door, which reads, "Good Night, GATH."

Below: The mausoleum as it looks today. No one was ever buried there.

Although his later letters to Genevieve make him sound alone and forlorn, GATH still had good times. In an undated letter to her, he mentioned receiving a note from the president, who was not named, but who asked him to come to the White House "at 9 last Friday night."

> *He had read my sketch of the election, which included him and was published Thursday. I went and found the whole evening was given to me, up to 11 o'clock, when I arouse myself. He sat with me in his study, wore diamond studs, etc. I had on two collar buttons at the wrists but wore the Paris dress suit. The president talked without reserve, said I was the only writer who grasped his character and the events around him and that he wanted me to come there whenever I wished and see him.*

Although there is no name or date to identify this president, there are other references in the letter to indicate that it was late in his life, probably after Bessie's death. It would be impossible to list all of the famous and important men and women he knew personally, but he knew several presidents before or at the time of their presidency during his lifetime. Theodore Roosevelt, Ulysses S. Grant, Rutherford B. Hayes, James A. Garfield and Chester A. Arthur were among them.

For many readers, his greatest gift was that of description of events and places, but he was at his best in describing not only the physical qualities of an individual but also incorporating the personality. It is worth noting just a few of those, written about people we still speak of today.

John Wilkes Booth

> *None of the printed pictures that I have seen do justice to Booth. He had one of the most vital heads I have ever seen. In fact, he was one of the best exponents of vital beauty I have ever met. By this I refer to physical beauty in the Medician sense—health, shapeliness, power in beautiful poise, and seemingly more powerful in repose than in energy. His hands and feet were sizable, not small, and his legs were stout and muscular, but inclined to bow like his father's. From the waist up, he was the perfect man, his chest being full and broad, his shoulders gently sloping and his arms as white as alabaster, but hard as marble. Over these, a neck which was its proper column rose the cornice of a fine Doric face, spare at the jaws and not anywhere over-ripe, but seamed with a nose of a Roman model, the only relic of his half-Jewish*

parentage, which gave decision to the thoughtfully stern sweep of two direct, dark eyes, meaning to woman snare, and to man a search warrant, while the lofty square forehead and square brows were crowned with a weight of curling jetty hair, like a rich Corinthian capital. His profile was eagleish and afar his countenance was haughty. He seemed thoughtful on introspections, ambitions self-examinings, eye-strides into the future, as if it withheld him something to which he had a right. I have since wondered whether moody demeanor did not come of a guilty spirit, but all Booths look so.

ABRAHAM LINCOLN AND STEPHEN A. DOUGLAS

Mr. Lincoln was a fine looking man, tall, well dressed, all ease and strength, the likeness of a new race upon the earth. Mr. Douglas was a Black Crook sort of man, a gnome, or Hermes, out of habits, though called a "judge." I went on the train with Lincoln, where he disappeared and turned up in Washington.

PRESIDENT JAMES A. GARFIELD

Garfield was and is a study. I think the religious bias was his weakness as a public man. He was a preaching professor. The natural man was first rate but subdued by Christian forbearance. He was a giant and full of courage but Ben Butler and others insulted him, knowing that the soft answer was his conscience. He was almost womanish in affection yet so shy that I was two or three years knowing him. When he thought he was obscure the country acclaimed him. He suffered Conkling's contumely like a coward and when he was shot, proved a dying Montezuma, saying, "If there is but one chance for life, we'll take that chance." Garfield had something of Lincoln.

JOHN BROWN, DEFINED

John Brown was an opinionated old giant, with tenacity and assertiveness of character, a Puritan in gravity and combativeness, experienced in the rougher portions of life and learned chiefly in odds and ends of things. His real life was martial and of the open air; his underlife was given to vague and disconnected philosophizing wherein he was variously a non-combatant in principle, a soldier of freedom and a martial poet, oppressed with the idea of uniting his philanthropy, his ambition and his love of turbulence in some great adventure.

JOHN BROWN AT HIS TRIAL

Sitting in court, John Brown looked like a colossal old bushwhacker; his long retreating head, shaped like one of his own pikes; his hair spiky, and his nose hooked, with deep indented nostrils; a forehead full of wrinkles, eyebrows pointed and projecting, and covered with grizzly wool, made up the rest of his features, and his neck was a column of bare muscle, his long legs were tucked into hide boots; he sat feeling his beard with his long digits, in an attitude that had the barest mock-heroic about it and there was a thoughtful genuineness in his expression that became his height and powers.

In a time when there were few photographs and no film or television, these powerful descriptions were much appreciated by those who read them. GATH was able to sum up with words both the physical appearance and the character and personality of his subjects.

GATH had many tributes made to him during his lifetime, and one of the best and most pleasing must have been this one, on his seventieth birthday by a longtime colleague and fellow journalist calling himself "Savoyard." In a 1911 article in the *Washington Evening Star* titled "Dean of the Cloth: George Alfred Townsend Heads Washington Correspondents," the writer offers profuse praise on the occasion of GATH's seventieth birthday:

George Alfred Townsend reached the age of three-score and ten years some days ago, and on that occasion received the congratulations and good wishes of numerous of his friends who gathered at his home for that purpose. The death of the veteran Shaw last year left Mr. Townsend the dean of that worthy cloth, Washington correspondents. He harks back McCullaugh, Piatt, Redfield, Ramsdel, Gibson, White, Richardson, Washington and others who made "letters" from Washington the cream of American journalism.

His versatility was boundless, his reading vast and varied, and his style captivating. He had both a passion and a genius for labor, and his physical as well as his mental constitution was stalwart, robust. He was prone to the discursive. He was also a strong partisan, though at one time he was supposed to be laboring under the malady of what subsequently became known as "mugwumpery," but in a very mild form.

I make no doubt that he was the most prolific writer our cloth has ever known. Daily he wrote thousands of words for newspapers, besides his steady stream of poetry, fiction and history. His physical strength must have been extraordinary and his industry ceaseless.

High praise, coming from his peers. GATH had many such honors during his lifetime, confirming his status in the community of writers. One of these was this notice in the *Washington Sentinel* on January 21, 1899:

George Alfred Townsend Mentioned as Potential Librarian of Congress

The death of the Hon. John Russell Young Tuesday creates a very desirable vacancy in the Government service which Mr. McKinley will be called upon to fill at an early date. The position of Librarian of Congress pays $6,000 a year and carries with it the control of considerable patronage. There will probably be a lively scramble for the place. Among the names that have already been mentioned in connection with the position are Representative Lemuel Ely Quigg, of New York; Gen. Henry V. Boynton; George Alfred Townsend; Thomas G. Alvord, and A.R. Spofford (sixth Librarian of Congress), 1864–1897.

A tribute in an obituary by William C. Hudson in the *Brooklyn Eagle* offers an accurate description of his career. Here is an excerpt:

For the greater part of his newspaper life, "Gath" was a singular figure. After he had secured his standing as a writer, he became an unattached worker—that is to say, unattached to the staff of any paper; but he continued his writing, and his copy was welcomed in widely separated papers. He rarely took assignments from any paper, and when he did it was for the specified time of some great event, and even then he may have been engaged for service to a dozen different papers. As an observant of any great event, no matter where occurring, he was quite certain to be found at work. The late Charles A. Dane, amused by his ubiquity, early christened him "the peripatetic journalist." He stood alone in this field, and though many attempted to occupy it with him, few if any succeeded.

As late as 1952, there were those who did not feel he deserved recognition but vilification. According to Shields, Augustus H. Able III, an English professor at the University of Delaware and a specialist in Delaware literature, "took it upon himself to savage Townsend's ambitions as a literary writer in a graduate lecture printed in 'Delaware Notes.' The tenor of Able's attack was that literature needed to be protected from upstarts like Townsend, who lacked the talent to qualify as a true literary artist." Despite this harsh opinion, Gath's *The Entailed Hat* has continued to be sought and read by knowledgeable Delaware book collectors.

His poetry was never very popular, and his newspaper columns are not widely available, but even now, visitors to Gathland's museum report having read some of his novels, which are still available on the Internet. His commentary, his newspaper "letters," were timely, to the point, interesting and widely read.

Shields concludes by commenting:

> *In his day however, he was a giant, familiar to most American newspaper readers, and a friend to many of the leading men of his era. The fact that many of his later literary writings have never been published, or even typed is a matter that could be easily remedied, and the recovery of much of his journalistic output is a task more easily accomplished in our present age of computers and scanners than it would have been earlier.*
>
> *Gath wanted his fellow Americans to learn the lessons a broad knowledge can teach. He has spent much of his life and energy trying to realize this goal. It would be a shame, after all his work, not to take advantage of it.*

Well said, Mr. Shields, and this part of his legacy is what this book hopes to convey to the reader.

Bessie's diabetes, the dropsy, the onset of blindness and general weakness and other symptoms of diabetes were taking a toll, and she was frequently in distress. GATH was attentive, though he was not always nearby; at the time of an especially bad spell, he was in Switzerland. He kept in close touch with his daughter Genevieve in New York, especially on the subject of her mother's health. In parts of this rather long letter to his daughter, GATH explains her condition, though not nearly in as much unpleasant detail as in later letters:

> *This beautiful Sunday, such weather as we have had for weeks, cool, temperate, leafy, birds singing, finds your mother unable to get out of bed.*

She has dropsy in the legs for two weeks, now in her thighs and face. She said yesterday, May 9, that she feared she would not go to Gapland. [Apparently this was written from their Washington home.] *She is settled that her end is near but talks little about it...Mrs. Townsend has taken a close interest in the painting of this house, finished today at a cost of $61. I have had her house at Gapland painted, especially the great porch where I expected to see her sitting. I have just gone in to see her fast asleep at nearly nine, as she lost much of the night from dysentery, eating rhubarb at supper. I think she sees a little, but little. I bought her a set of cottage English china for $12 yesterday. Dr. Robbins says that she will probably die of dropsy on the lungs; her diarrheas are frequent, especially at nights, she has no caution about eating. I hope that Mrs. Townsend can be got to Gapland but Dr. Robbins says the city for physicians and drugs is much better for her.*

Bessie's illness was long and unpleasant, but GATH seemed to maintain a loyal presence and demonstrates, as evidenced in his letters, a genuine affection for her. But depression was inevitable, as he, too, was getting older and more infirm.

Later in the letter, he includes an update on his son, Alfred Jr., who had been a constant disappointment and worry, even more for Bessie than for GATH. There is no mention of anything good Alfred Jr. had done or become; the few references to him are always negative:

Alfred Townsend has lost his place, I think through the extravagance, vanity and softening of the brain, his employer who is uncertain and in debt. In addition, Alfred has kidney complaint and is ordered to quit all worry. Faithful to his toys, he owns an automobile. He has a few hundred dollars; I have a thousand. When I married I had $900; thus do the two ends of life about balance.

In 1903, Bessie died. A marker currently at the site of the former estate in Western Maryland states that he became a virtual recluse when his wife died—a bit too glib on the part of that writer, who apparently has never been elderly. GATH did not become a recluse but rather a man in his late sixties, suffering from diabetes, gout and lack of funds and whose wife had died after a long and difficult illness. His lifestyle reflected that. He continued to travel to Gapland and visit with his daughter and grandchildren, as well as relatives and friends in Washington. And he continued to write, though not for publication.

He complained in letters to Genevieve, this one a month after Bessie's death:

All things seem to descend from cause. But ambition is a delusion. These great modern times despise egotism and the ability of the hand has whipped the ability of the head. I hope I may not live too long alone.

I have been four days at Gapland, sleeping remote from anybody. Nobody has called. Today I did the disquieting work of cleaning out your mother's desk, full of letters, many from you. Death is made miserable by the avidity of the living. A nest of robins is in the woodbin on the porch, the old bird screaming to see my approach as if I were death. I go out and whistle to the birds to assure them, but a sob ends the whistling. My wife had been so long dependent that I feel as I had dropped a happy grief. I have lived too long in the illusions of fame which are now nothing.

Later that year, he wrote:

I go out but little; am tempted to drink and gab when I do. At nine every night I am in bed. My servant is old mammy like, but kind; talks too much and gets set down upon.

I ordered my lawyer to have your brother deed my Mt. Gath property back, or I would sue him at Hagerstown for improper influence over a weak-minded wife. He and his wife made haste to obey. That is all.

He writes to his daughter, Genevieve, late in his life a comment on an issue now becoming current again and a comment on his feelings for Bessie and their marriage:

For two months we have had practically no servants; the leveling of everybody up to the rich line, has included the poor, who do not want to work. I cannot see much quality in life when a man does his own work and a woman must have 2 other women to do hers. We begin to perceive that domestic slavery had its uses for both master and servant. Our black women are worthless; our white women will not work in kitchens. Labor is very scarce in the country. How poor would be the universal wealth, compelled to do its own drudging.

Your mother is as always, rather better in temper, workful but weak. It is not impossible that I may die first, as I am full of blood, and she drained of it. It is an issue between apoplexy and diabetes. She would be a great loss to me, notwithstanding our divergencies. Early attachment is stronger than many pulls away.

Gradually, to meet his expenses, some of his possessions were sold off. Two auctions were held in March and April 1909 by C.F. Libbie & Co. of Boston. The library was so extensive that the auction was scheduled over a period of three days. The catalogue cover reads:

VALUABALE PRIVATE LIBRARY of GEORGE ALFRED TOWNSEND, History. Social Life in European Capitals, Dramatic Lincolniana and Wilkes Booth, John Brown of Harpers Ferry, Southern and Western History. Extra Illustrated Books, Curiosa, Pennsylvania and German Imprints, Indians, New York City and State, Maryland History and Imprints, etc.

The second auction promised "Autograph Collection, Rare Etchings and Engravings, Water Colors and Oil Paintings, Curiosa, etc." It noted that "most of the autographs refer to important matters in our history and were addressed to Mr. Townsend during their occurrence. They therefore have a value above souvenirs."

In a letter to his daughter, GATH writes, "I sent 100 to your husband as Edmund left. For all my books and things I received not till May 21 net, 2,406—out of $4,731—the advertising was $305, catalogue $565, (illegible) $79, and postage, etc., so that Libbie (the auction house) got $2,325 and I got $240."

It must have been even more painful than his persistent illnesses for GATH so see his beloved library and his collected art treasures sold. Another auction was held in October 1912. "Many Attend Sale of 'GATH's' Belongings," announced the *Valley Register* in Middletown, Maryland:

Some 600 or 800 people attended the sale last Tuesday of the personal effects at Gapland, South Mountain, of Mr. Geo. Alfred Townsend, the novelist and correspondent. Many came from Frederick, Hagerstown and all sections of the valley, while some were present from Baltimore, Frederick, Hagerstown, New York and elsewhere. There were nearly fifty automobiles on the grounds. Hundreds of valuable curios, picked up by the correspondent in his world wanderings, were sold at good prices. Much valuable furniture, pictures, bric-a-brac etc., however, went at a great sacrifice. The sale was one of the most interesting ever held in the valley, and was continued on Wednesday. The buildings and land were not offered at public sale. A private bid of $10,000 was scorned by Mr. Townsend.

Ten years would go by before it sold, and then for no more than he had scoffed at in 1912. The loss of his wife, estrangement from son and his increasing infirmities drained his spirit. His sinking station in life and the depletion of his finances were a constant torment, and his despondency persisted. He struggled to stay the course. In 1910, he wrote to his daughter, "I went New Year's to Mrs. Howard's reception. Mrs. Atkins was there, twice her former size." He continues:

> *I am often lonesome, go to bed too early, do not get about enough but am writing another story. My head survives my hams, which discourages exercise. My opera box is my bed. I live in four rooms, the parlor-secretary, the whiskey retiring room, the basement refectory and the bedroom. There is no way to make Age bully but to cuddle down. My fancy booth is my front window, and I shall be recollected as the old scribbling hermit, sitting there imagining. Visitors do not go well with preoccupation. But, adieu, as my pipe is full.*

In his memoirs, which he began in 1913 but never completed, GATH tells us the end of his story at great length; the fame, the fortune, the famous and the obscure, the thrill of it all. But the most telling part is in the beginning, when he writes:

> *I have just passed my 73rd year and feel lost without some writing to do, as I have been almost continuously writing public information or literature since my twelfth or thirteenth year. Three score years of pushing the quill as the exponent of my hand have become second nature and I hardly understand why I am not still wanted.*

On another occasion, watching the era in which he had taken such a prominent part, and seeing the people who shared it with him fade from the stage, he remarks, "I cannot understand how I could be so quickly forgotten." For all his success, his vast intellect, his cocoon of worldly goods, it appeared he would now be consigned to oblivion. But he had a plan. And it worked. He is once again remembered, sometimes disparaged but usually admired. He is still a player.

9

THE ARCH EXPLAINED

*A*round 1894, during Bessie's long illness and his own decline, GATH began to plan the War Correspondents Memorial. Following the pattern of his previous buildings, he first sketched the design he wanted, then consulted with an architect to refine it and, finally, supervised the building of the Arch. This would be his last project, and it must serve as the crowning achievement and eternal reminder to everything he had accomplished.

As he had done with all his previous buildings, he first sketched his design, taken partly from the Antietam Fire House in Hagerstown; added the arch from the Hagerstown Railroad Station; and then included embellishments such as the terra cotta representations of Greek mythology, quotations from famous people in history and other flourishes of his creative and artistic imagination. Then it went to the architect for proper rendering and then to construction.

By now, with no funds of his own, GATH found it necessary to stage a vast and very successful fundraising campaign, writing letters to present and former acquaintances asking for help in building the monument. It is not known how many such letters were sent, but it is a tribute to his good name and reputation that more than thirty years after the Civil War, he was able to raise $5,000 for the project. The ability to raise the money to erect the monument speaks of respect for not only war correspondents but also GATH himself.

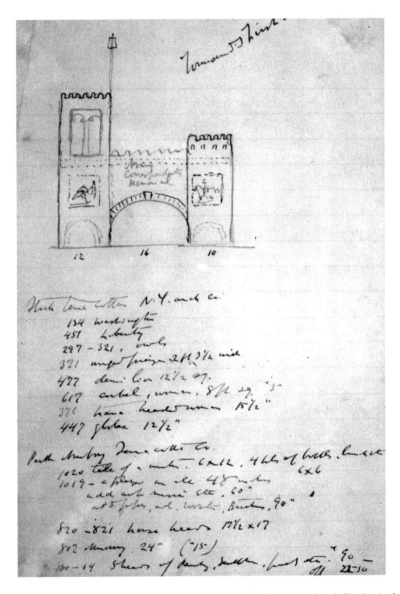

Above: Townsend designed all of the buildings at Gapland. This is the sketch for the Arch, which was the first step in all Townsend's designs for buildings. They then went to an architect for rendering. The design came to him while standing in the Hagerstown Railroad station and looking across the street at the Antietam Fire Company building. Features of the railroad station also contributed to the design of the Arch.

Opposite, top: The architect's blueprint for the Arch.

Opposite, bottom: The Arch under construction. Townsend designed it, raised the funds and had it constructed in record time.

GATH, speaking to an unnamed reporter, stated:

Thirty one years after the war I built the only War Correspondents' Memorial in the world at my residence on Crampton's Gap, South Mountain battle field, at a cost of over $5,000. Seeing at Hagerstown a horseshow arch and fire engine tower of limestone, I assembled them and three upper Roman arches in a screen 50 feet high by forty wide, below one large Moorish arch, sixteen feet height and span, above nine feet arches flanked by a tower, the whole battlemented. I had seen at Pontassieve in Italy fine effects of moonlight in high gateways. The Moorish arch and horses' heads typified the horseshoe that carried the rider from battle. Two slabs in the rear had the names of all the writers and artists I could hear of cut, and at the ends were texts from the battle writers of antiquity and part of my own poem called the "War Correspondent's Last Ride."

Contributors were many and among them the names of John Wannamaker, George Pullman, Joseph Pulitzer, Thomas Edison, P. Studebaker and J. Pierpont Morgan. Writers and journalists are also prevalent. Corporations such as the Baltimore and Ohio Railroad, the Pennsylvania Railroad and the Western Maryland and Reading Railroads were supporters. Several major newspapers also supported the effort. Contributions ranged from $25 to $200.

A bugler and drummer from the Washington Barracks were provided by the Adjutant General's Office of the War Department, "provided the government is not put to any expense thereby; and that instructions have been sent to the Commanding General, Department of the East."

Maryland governor Lloyd Lowndes officiated at the 1896 dedication, along with the directors of the Army War Correspondents Memorial: Whitelaw Reid, Albert D. Richardson, W.H. Rankle, O.G. Sawyer, W.F.G. Shanks, R.H. Shelly, George W. Smalley, Henry M. Stanley, Edmund C. Stedman, Jerome B. Stillson, W.H. Stiner, William Swinton, R.H. Sylvester, Benjamin F. Taylor, George Alfred Townsend, B.C. Truman, Henry Villard, J.H. Vosbug, E.W. Wollaz, J.S. Ward, Sam Ward, F. Watson, E.D Westfall, F.B. Wilkie, Sam Wilkerson, F. Wilkerson, F. Wilkison, A.W. Williams, J.C. Wilson, T.C. Wilson, J.R. Young, W. Young.

The work began on the fifth anniversary of Lincoln's death and was dedicated on the anniversary of John Brown's raid on Harpers Ferry. The dedication took place on October 16, 1896, and as GATH intended, it was a splendid affair. Townsend began a lengthy address with this introduction:

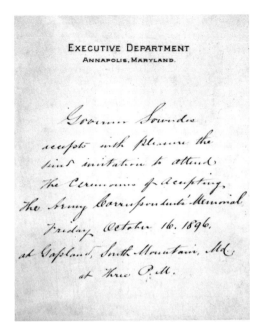

Left: Letter of acceptance from then-governor of Maryland Lowndes to the invitation to appear at the Dedication of the War Correspondents Memorial.

Below: A grocery bill for items purchased for the dedication of the Arch, which lists port, rum, vermouth, beer, baked beans in sauce, smoked tongue, sardines and soda crackers.

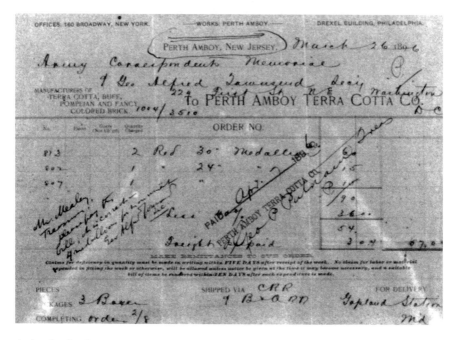

An invoice for the terra cotta Townsend used for decorative elements on his structures.

Comrade Correspondents, Friends: Like the universe, this monument has evolved. Twenty years after the war, one of the army reporters still entranced with the campaign themes of his boyhood, found his way to this naked spot as the scene of a conflict he desired to use in a romance. Where he stopped and stood, an apparently unprofitable arrival to the laborers along the mountainside and the farmers in the valleys beneath him, now arises this memorial thirty-one years after the war.

Its lesson to the neighbors around it is the profitableness of knowledge and of letters and imagination to any people, however they may undervalue these things. That uncommercial traveler found things to do: wells to strike, rocks to subdue, men to enlist, roads to create. The busy human head is also a farm, and engine and a shop.

Twelve years of pleasant contention with nature and rusticity has multiplied objects in this old battle gap when, like the image of Diana appearing to King Pericles in the play, and saying, "Perform my bidding or thou livest in woe; Do't and be happy, by my silver bow" and the apparition of this monument suddenly arose to the aging correspondent.

The dedication was set down for the *Washington Evening Star* in an editorial by Crosby S. Noyes, a fellow journalist and friend:

The Unique Monument at Gapland.

A monument unique in design and location, as well as in what it commemorates, was formally dedicated today at Gapland, Maryland. It is a memorial to the army correspondents and artists of the war, who wrote and illustrated the daily history of the great conflict. With the war and the war correspondent and the great demand by the public for information came the wonderful modern development of the American newspaper. The war was epoch-making in newspaper offices as well as in national councils. So the memorial at Gapland is something more than a monument to the memory of individuals. It marks the advance in journalism in which the American newspaper has led the world. Its location looking down from the mountain side over the wide Maryland valleys and the historic Potomac, the scene of much of the stirring panorama of the civil war, was happily chosen. The newer generations of journalists must ever revere the memory of the men whose enterprise, persistence under untold difficulties, personal daring and literary ability, won for their calling a prestige that has done much to inspire every newspaper worker with a pride in his craft. The addresses made today will be found most readable, for they bring graphically to view again much that was of fascinating interest in war history, the daily life, the trials and achievements of those who had to be always at the front—the war reporter.

The monument is indeed an unusual, very large and handsome tribute. Hindes's description appears almost everywhere, probably because it is most accurate, and it is reproduced here:

In appearance the monument is quite odd. It is fifty feet high and forty feet broad. Above a Moorish arch sixteen feet high built of Hummelstown purple stone are super-imposed three Roman arches. These are flanked on one side with a square crenellated tower, producing a bizarre and picturesque effect. Niches in different places shelter the carving of two horses' heads, and symbolic terra cotta statuettes of Mercury, Electricity and Poetry. Tables under the horses' heads bear the suggestive words "Speed" and "Heed": the heads are over the Roman arches. The three roman arches are made of limestone from Creek Battlefield, Virginia, and each nine feet high and six feet wide. These arches represent Description, Depiction and Photography.

The aforementioned tower contains a statue of Pan with the traditional pipes, and he is either half drawing or sheathing a roman sword. Over a small turret on the opposite side of the tower is a gold vane of a pen bending a sword. At various places on the monument are quotations appropriate to the art of war correspondence. These are from a great variety of sources beginning with the Old Testament verses. Perhaps the most striking feature of all are the tablets inscribed with the names of 157 correspondents and war artists who saw and described in narrative and picture almost all the events of the four years of the war.

GATH's statements on the Arch were, like his comments on his Gapland estate, factual and unemotional:

The war correspondents' monument is the least expensive structure for its extended impression in the country. There are monuments in Washington whose pedestals cost six times its whole expenditure. It was also the fleetest enterprise on any upon our battlefields—finished within nine months of its conception. Ten feet of its solid height is invisible in the foundations. It has been art school to the stonemasons of the countryside.

The names of one hundred and seven Union army correspondents are recorded alphabetically upon the tall tablet in the north rear of the memorial, and nine southern correspondents (all of them which we could verify), are placed in the south rear, the latter between two divisions of pictorial correspondents, numbering in all thirty-six.

More anxiety to have fellow craftsmen omitted than recognized sometimes sought to direct us, but we searched the three pictorial newspapers of the war-time and thus extended the list of artists which we had been led to believe were all named in our lower or second tabulation.

No person is omitted, whatever his misfortune in later life; the only question we asked was, "Did he serve in this function of relating and drawing war events and scenes for the public information?"

The weather vane, one of many personal reminders GATH put on the monument, was another descriptor of the man who built it. A replica of the weather vane, designed by GATH, can be seen in the Gathland Park Museum.

"The pen is mightier than the sword" was coined by Edward Bulwer-Lytton for his 1839 play *Richelieu, or the Conspiracy*:

The weather vane Townsend designed for the tower of the Arch, "The Pen Is Mightier than the Sword." A copy of it is in the museum at Gathland. *Photo by author.*

> *True, This!—Beneath the rule of men entirely great, The pen is mightier than the sword. Behold The arch-enchanters wand!—itself a nothing!—But taking sorcery from the master-hand To paralyse the Caesars, and to strike The loud earth breathless!—Take away the sword—States can be saved without it!*

This may have been the source for GATH's use of the phrase, but some derivation of the concept has been used through the ages, beginning in ancient Greece. The first example came from the Greek playwright Euripides, who is said to have written, "The tongue is mightier than the blade," and later the Islamic prophet Muhammad is quoted as saying, "The ink of the scholar is holier than the blood of the martyr."

These lines from Gath's poem "Building" written on the monument, identify his architecture as an extension of his writing:

> *The bookman's art is left behind*
> *And letters only vex.*
> *Write then in stone, ye minds of men!*
> *And live as architects!*

To the Army Correspondents and Artists 1861–65 Whose Toils Cheered the Camps, Thrilled the Fireside, Educated Provinces of Rustics into a Bright Nation of Readers, and Gave Incentive to Narrate Distant Wars and Explore Dark Lands
Erected by Subscription 1896

O wondrous youth Through this grand ruth
Runs my boy's life, its thread
The General's fame, the battle's name
The rolls of maimed and dead
I bear with my thrilled soul astir
And lonely thoughts and fears
And am but history's courier
To bind the conquering years
A battle's ray, through ages gray
To light to deeds sublime
And flash the lustre of my day
Down all the aisles of time

War Correspondents' Ballad, 1865

With its overwhelming size, European design of mixed antiquity, variously colored stone and terra cotta–colored embellishments, inscribed marble tablets and mythological figures, it was indeed a spectacular creation. Even now, it appears without warning, majestically crowning the crest of a hill in its rustic and rural setting. Like GATH, it is larger than life, heavily embellished and more than a little flamboyant. It is truly monumental. The monument is richly covered with symbolic architectural detail. It is inexplicable to most, and many writers have tried to interpret the symbols he integrated into the structure.

GATH admitted that his overall design was an amalgam of the Arch at the Hagerstown Railroad Station and the towers on the Antietam fire hall across the street. The use of mythology might have baffled the average person, but GATH was well acquainted with the gods and goddesses of Greek and Roman antiquity and used them appropriately to send his message. Unfortunately, many visitors did not understand it, and there has always been wildly inaccurate conjecture about the identity of and the meaning of the figures displayed on the Arch. GATH describes the south face:

The Antietam Fire Company building in Hagerstown, which inspired Townsend's design for the Arch.

The South end contains quotes from Thucydides, Xenophon, Froissart, Philip de Commines, Benjamin Franklin, George Washington, General Sheridan, Henry M. Stanley and McGahan. The two faces of the arch are dramatically different. The South face seems to perfectly express war correspondents; plain to the point of austerity, unadorned with color or artistic flourishes. The names of the correspondents who wrote about the war and the artists who sketched it for the newspapers are etched into marble slabs mounted on the wall.

The other side is quite a different presentation entirely. It is heavily embellished (a word Townsend used in reference to his other structures as well), colorful, flamboyant and impressive.

According to Hindes, the terra cotta busts represent Electricity and Poetry, and the statue in the tower niche is Pan. The three open arches at the top of the monument represent Description, Depiction and Photography. A much more recent description names the statue "either Orpheus or Pheidippides," and the busts are "believed to be Mercury and Apollo." Since none of these figures was created specifically for this project, but rather purchased from a manufacturer of outdoor sculpture and ornamentation, they were meant to represent gods and goddesses. The same is true of the dog that sat on top of the mausoleum; it was intended to represent a guard dog GATH might have owned.

Here are descriptions from Patrick Hiatt, a Frederick artist who frequently paints modern versions of Greek and Latin myths and who has done the research:

The statue (in the niche) is actually a copy of a very popular and often copied sculptural work created by the artist Bertel Thorvaldsen in 1818, "Mercury About to Kill Argus." While most people associate the reed pipes with Pan, it was actually Hermes (the Greek name for Mercury) who invented the pipes as a part of his disguise used in his plot to kill the giant Argus. His symbolic use of Thorvaldsen's Mercury rather than the traditional figure of Mars for war probably relates to the youth of those who fight in wars, rather than just the act of war.

The medallion on the left is Mercury, with his winged cap and a Roman caduceus. Townsend's words from his "War Correspondent Ballad," inscribed on the Monument's North side, are significantly focused on youth. Townsend, who had an immense ego, may also have used this sculpture because he saw himself, like Mercury, as a courier and messenger of the gods. The medallion on the right is Erato, the muse of lyric poetry and one of nine goddesses in Greek mythology who control the nine types of art known to ancient Greece. Townsend's use of Erato is appropriate since he was a poet and an author. The muse was typically invoked at or near the beginning of an ancient poem or classical Greek hymn and she also served as an aid to authors of prose.

All of the sculptures are cast concrete and are probably American made copies commissioned by Townsend. European copies at the time were usually carved from marble or cast in plaster and were more refined but very expensive and difficult to acquire. Concrete would also survive the elements better. The medallions were painted to resemble terracotta.

In all the descriptions that exist, no one has quite known what to do with the shields bearing the words "Speed" and "Heed." It's a safe guess that Speed refers to the necessity of getting news published quickly, and a few journalists ventured that Heed could refer to paying attention to the truth, or the rules of journalism.

Isolated as it is from the main thoroughfares, the Arch has had a long and sometimes contentious history. Mary Carter-Roberts (1899–1979) was a journalist and novelist. She took an interest in the monument in the late 1950s and found it quite forgotten. She relates that the monument was not on the list of National Park areas, and no one in the park service knew anything about it. After contacting a member of the Maryland Board of Natural Resources, she said the U.S. government admitted that it owned the monument and considered it part of Antietam National Battlefield Park. She wrote:

Lost indeed. Not only is it absent from the records, there are no signs directing one to it, no explanation of its history when one gets there. One comes along the road to the top of the mountain, and there it is. Alone among the trees. An unidentified phenomenon, save as the names of great writers utter their silent shout from the stone face. This, after more than half a century of federal ownership.

Local residents familiar with the monument knew it only as the "War Correspondents' Monument," and some remember that long period during which it stood neglected as the rest of the property was disintegrating. The federal government has owned it since 1904, when GATH gave it to the War Department. It was later transferred to the federal Parks Department, administered out of nearby Antietam, and while it is pristine today, apparently it was quite shabby for some time. When heritage tourism became popular, and Civil War sites and battlefields became huge attractions, the monument was suddenly in the spotlight again.

The War Correspondents Memorial Arch, designed by GATH with John L. Smithmeyer as architect, was said to be the only such tribute to war correspondents in the world at the time of its construction. It is certainly the largest. However, at Arlington National Cemetery, there is a small marble tribute, formed in the shape of a book, lying on the ground in front of a specially planted tree. The inscription reads:

WAR CORRESPONDENTS

This tree grows in memory of journalists who died while covering wars or conflicts for the American people. One who finds a truth lights a torch.

In Remembrance
No Greater Love
Overseas Press Club
Society of Professional Journalists (Sigma Delta Chi)
The National Press Club
October 7, 1986

One other site honoring war correspondents is located inside of the Newseum in Washington, D.C. At this location, white translucent squares, one for each correspondent, hang back-lit at a huge window. Unlike the Arch, correspondents are not admitted to this memorial until they are dead, and their deaths must have occurred in the service of their jobs as journalists.

Though the Arch is still relatively unknown, the Appalachian Trail has brought many thousands of visitors to the site, surprising them with its grandeur in this unlikely location. Also on the Appalachian Trail is the Washington Monument, located just nine miles away, another very local monument. Built by the citizens of Boonsboro in 1827, it is a cairn-like structure poised high above the Middletown valley. Local citizens worked until noon on July 4 of that year and then held a dedication ceremony and lunch. They resumed work and by 4:00 p.m. the monument stood fifteen feet high on a fifty-four-foot circular base. The day ended with the reading of the Declaration of Independence and a three-round salute fired by three Revolutionary War veterans. The workers returned that September to finish the monument. Over the years, it fell into disrepair and was repaired by a men's civic organization; still later, it was completely rebuilt by the Civilian Conservation Corps. If GATH's Arch is a tribute to the courage and bravery of war correspondents, the Washington Monument honors not only George Washington, but also the patriotic spirit of the men and women of Boonsboro who built it.

Once again, GATH had his critics, and a local writer and un-credentialed historian wannabe savaged him thoroughly in an article written in 2003 because of the author's personal opposition to the inclusion of war correspondents who were killed in the Iraq conflict and were memorialized with a marker at the site in spite of his protests.

His ostensible basis for protesting the concept is his claim that he is the unofficial historian of Crampton's Gap, the site of a Civil War battle and of the Arch. He claims that title for having devoted twenty years of his life to research and dissemination of the site's history. He is indignant that GATH, whom he describes as an "eccentric, shameless self-promoter," has seen fit to desecrate the battlefield site with his grandiose buildings. He is certain that GATH selected the site for his home, and later the Arch, to propel himself to immortality with his maudlin novel *Katy of Catoctin*. He states that the "Townsend epoch" has been "allowed to smother the battlefield itself, suffocating the site with his own ego."

The writer attempts to "prove," one hundred years after the monument was created, that the list of 157 names honored on the Arch was compiled with unmistakable personal bias. He claims that 33 of them cannot be identified. Approximately 22 have no business being there at all, being Townsend's personal friends, large contributors to the project or persons with whom Townsend wished to ingratiate himself. Many names are absent, incomplete, misspelled or misstated. Some southern journalists were omitted due to his bitter anti-southern bias, according to that writer.

Finally, because he considers the Crampton's Gap to be so defiled by the intrusion of dead war correspondents, he pushed the Maryland legislature to introduce a bill in the 2004 session that would change the name to Crampton's Gap State Battlefield Park, to "[arrest] once and for all Townsend's misuse of the site."

So far, this has not occurred.

At the time he conceived and built the Arch, Townsend knew that his illustrious career, his writing and even his lovingly created estate would not live on. He observed Mark Twain's career blossoming into the twentieth century, aware that his would not. Twain became famous for his books and

An early photo of the road leading to the Arch.

stories, written after he left his newspaper career. GATH's novels never caught fire as Twain's did. His children had made it plain that they would not attempt to preserve his property or his legacy and that he would not be buried in the mausoleum he had built.

In his memoirs, begun in 1913, a year before his death, Townsend bemoans the fact that he is being forgotten. And as he feared, he was hardly more than a footnote in the occasional book.

Except for the Arch.

The Arch has had many celebrations in the one hundred years since GATH's death in 1914 and they are listed in the Epilogue.

EPILOGUE

*N*o stated reasons come down to us as to why Bessie, and later GATH, were not buried in the crypt he had built. Since visiting the graves of loved ones was more common then, it is possible that the distance relatives would have had to travel to visit the graves seemed prohibitive. Another practical consideration was the painful fact that even at the time of Bessie's death in 1903, GATH knew that the property would not stay in the family and the crypt would be owned by strangers. There is no truth to the story that GATH's father and mother were buried in the tomb and later moved. No one was ever buried there.

Two feature articles appeared in the *Baltimore Sun* years after Gapland was sold, one by Betty M. Snyder in December 1925 and one in September 1936 by Harry Haller. Snyder's work is so riddled with erroneous statements that it is impossible to trust what could be correct. Unfortunately, it probably has been used in research by later authors, perpetuating the errors for future historians.

Haller's 1936 article is much more accurate and better conveys the spirit of the place and the haunting mythical atmosphere that enveloped it then. Nor did he resort to the often used words "bizarre" and "eccentric," which are poor and inaccurate descriptions of the man and his creations. Many curious tales were inspired by the legendary GATH and his fanciful buildings, and they lend themselves to wild imaginings. As time blurs our recollections, myth grows around them.

By 1936, the time of Haller's story, the property had been abandoned for more than twenty years. Due to vandalism—and outright theft—of all the

The Arch as it appears today.

fine materials and ornamentation that GATH left behind, the buildings were ravaged. Haller's observations bring a different dimension from those who were present when GATH was there to welcome the visitor:

> *Only a literary man could have conceived the odd set up that resulted. Rooms were built with apparently no regard for light, entrances and exits and other utilitarian purposes, but merely at the whim of the builder. Some of them are almost completely cut off from the rest of the house; some are all windows and others must have been constantly in semi-darkness. With a predominance of the Victorian influence, the exteriors seem to hold neither rhyme nor reason. Gothic spires clash with absurdly set Roman arches, Moorish turrets and great rambling porches. One of the doorways was entered through a portico copied from Washington Irving's Sunnyside-on-the-Hudson, another is in pure Colonial style, and others in equally discordant styles.*
>
> *Here and there, high near the roof of a building or stuck away under a porch one finds quotations from the classics engraved on marble. There seems to be no particular pertinency to any of them, but imagination has led people to devise various interpretations. For instance, Townsend's use of Ezekiel's words, "I sought a man who should stand in the Gap before me for the Land," carved on a slab fronting the home in which he lived, might have several significances.*

The *Frederick Daily News* reported on April 27, 1914:

> *By a deed filed at the clerk's office for record in the Washington County Court Saturday, the late George Alfred Townsend, better known as "Gath," transferred to his son-in-law, Edmund F. Bonaventure, his beautiful country estate of 100 acres at Gapland, Washington County, buildings, furniture, vehicles, etc. Seventy-five acres of the property are in Washington County and twenty-five in Frederick County.*

Bonaventure died in 1918, but Genevieve did not sell the property until 1920, for $9,500, a tiny fraction of its cost. Several sources claim that GATH spent $500,000 on Gapland, but in the archives, he claimed an amount closer to $200,000, still an imposing sum given the value of the dollar in 1890. And he does not indicate that the cost of his accumulated art treasures, silver, china, antiques, home furnishings and especially his cherished library are included in that amount; certainly, the costs of these would bring the total well over half a million dollars.

The new owner, James Reid, attempted to create an inn of some kind at Gapland Hall, but he failed to make it work. A recent visitor to the museum said that her mother had worked there for a while as an innkeeper but wasn't sure how long Reid's endeavor lasted.

According to a 1939 feature in the *Washington Star* on the now crumbling estate, Teina C. Fisher of Baltimore, Maryland, who inherited a mortgage on the property, and Virginia Lee Siebert of Silver Spring, Maryland, bought the property for $750 at a tax sale. Another source says it was Mrs. Siebert who inherited the mortgage, but they seemed to have jointly purchased it.

Still deteriorating steadily by the elements—aided by vandals and scavengers—the property fell to further ruin. In 1943, the Maryland and Virginia Eldership of the Churches of God bought the property from Mrs. Fisher for a reported $1,500, intending to restore it as a church home for the aged and a conference and retreat center. By 1947 they, too, had abandoned the project and offered it for sale.

Askelon, the first house built at Gapland, around 1946. It is no longer in existence. *Courtesy Aubrey Bodine.*

The Lodge, with kitchen extensions, around 1946. The original stone building is now a museum depicting the Civil War Battle that was fought in 1862 at this site. *Courtesy Aubrey Bodine.*

In 1946, a rededication celebration was held for the fiftieth anniversary of the building of the Arch, which was attended by Townsend and Bonaventure descendants. Also in 1946, a proposal to add the names of Ernie Pyle, Louis Creel and other World War II correspondents was not approved. Records don't show exactly who vetoed that idea, but the Churches of God still owned the land at that time.

In the 1930s, the Appalachian Trail was completed in the area. The Gapland site was exactly the sort of contribution the creators of the trail had envisioned would be made by the states through which it passed, buffering the trail with recreational land. Local civic-minded citizens from Frederick County purchased the land at a tax sale, paying $3,800 for the 110 acres and the ruined buildings, which they gave to the State of Maryland. The Arch remains the property of the federal government, which has maintained it since Townsend donated it in 1904. It is maintained by staff at the nearby Antietam National Park.

1950 DATA AND RECOMMENDATION SURVEY FOR GATHLAND STATE PARK:

Since October 16, 1946, Robert E. Delaplaine, owner of the News *and the* Post *in Frederick, had advocated return of the historically valuable site to the public.*

Ten public-spirited citizens in Frederick headed by Elmer I. Eshleman, past president of the Frederick Chamber of Commerce and executive officer of the Western Maryland Bank, arranged to purchase the 100 acres of the estate for approximately $3,500 in 1948. These individuals gave the deed to the land over to the state, and by passing a bid from a private contractor for the building materials on the property, sold at a discount the restorable buildings and habitations to Maryland, with a proviso of Historical collaboration in the rest of the buildings. The 1949 session of the Maryland legislature appropriated $10,000 in Public Improvement Funds, for restoration of the estate as Gathland State Park.

Sadly, forty years of neglect, vandalism and the ravages of weather left almost nothing salvageable among Townsend's once-splendid buildings. The citizens' group, consisting of members of the Frederick Chamber of Commerce and the Historical Society of Frederick County, stipulated that the State Forest and Parks Department should first clear the land to provide safe recreational hiking and other recreational pursuits, develop a suitable water supply to meet public demand, establish a guardianship to conserve what is left and supervise primary restoration of fundamental necessities.

Finally, the goal was to restore and make available to public visitation and/or use the Crypt, Carriage House, Gapland Hall, Den and Library, Barn and small cottage in front of Gapland and remove the guest cottage of frame construction now in bad condition. It was a tall order, and one that, due partly to lack of funding and partly to the badly deteriorated condition of the buildings, could not be fully accomplished. The new park was dedicated in 1958.

A report by Robert L. Lagemann, a park historian of the Antietam National Battlefield Site, on May 18, 1961, states:

Before his death, Townsend had in 1904, given the memorial arch and the property on which it sat, to the Federal Government, and was managed by the

Top: The condition of Gapland Hall around 1955. *Courtesy Walter Dippold.*

Bottom: Gapland Hall, looking badly deteriorated. After acquiring the property in 1949, the Department of Natural Resources renovated just one segment of this building for the museum now at Gathland.

War Department. By the time this property was transferred to the National Park Service in August of 1933, the other portions of the estate had changed hands a number of times and had fallen into dereliction. Since then, the other properties continued to change hands and to further deteriorate until 1948 when the State of Maryland acquired it and established Gathland State Park at the Gap. The War Correspondents Memorial Arch at Crampton's Gap now has the status of a federally owned park entirely surrounded by a state owned and operated park.

During the 1960s, then-governor J. Millard Tawes proposed creating a newspaper hall of fame at the site. It was a huge, futuristic design and not considered appropriate to the site. The Maryland-Delaware Press Association drafted a plan that included an amphitheater built into the hillside just below the Arch. The proposal faded into oblivion, never to return, when funds to build it were not available and support did not materialize. No attempt has been made to revive it.

As the park began to take shape in the 1970s with a small museum created in the Lodge by Gerry Sword, a parks manager who emphasized historical interpretation of the parks he managed. Increased historical interpretation was begun in the 1980s with the efforts of Department of Natural Resources staff members Ralph Young and Ross Kimmel.

Journalism activities continued to develop the site. On October 11, 1974, Sigma Delta Chi, the Society of Professional Journalists, honored Townsend as a Civil War correspondent, novelist and poet.

HISTORIC SITE IN JOURNALISM
HONORING
GEORGE A. TOWNSEND

Civil War correspondent, Novelist and Poet, constructed this War Correspondents Arch in 1896 as a memorial to the 157 correspondents and Artists of the North and South who reported on the Civil War. It is the only known memorial to newspapermen in the world.

Marked this 11th day of October, 1974.

This plaque is in the Gathland museum at the site of the War Correspondents' Memorial Arch.

The Friends of Gathland State Park formed in 1992 under the leadership of park manager Dan Spedden and led by volunteer Marge Magruder. The Friends put up exhibits related to GATH and his family and estate in the part of Gapland Hall that had been renovated. The Friends of Gathland State Park was merged with the South Mountain Battlefield State Park. The group staged public events to raise funds and created multiple projects to enhance the museum.

Budget cuts forced a shutdown of the park in 1991, and it was reopened in 1994 through the efforts of the Friends of South Mountain Battlefield.

In 1996, a celebration of the 100th anniversary of the building of the Arch attracted dignitaries and descendants, including members of the Rasmussen family, descendants of GATH's daughter, Genevieve Townsend Bonaventure.

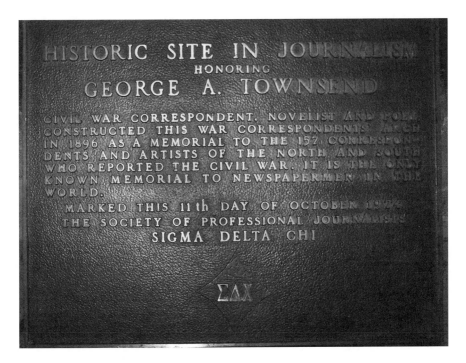

HISTORIC SITE IN JOURNALISM
HONORING
GEORGE A. TOWNSEND

CIVIL WAR CORRESPONDENT, NOVELIST AND POET, CONSTRUCTED THIS WAR CORRESPONDENTS' ARCH IN 1896 AS A MEMORIAL TO THE 157 CORRESPONDENTS AND ARTISTS OF THE NORTH AND SOUTH WHO REPORTED THE CIVIL WAR. IT IS THE ONLY KNOWN MEMORIAL TO NEWSPAPERMEN IN THE WORLD.
MARKED THIS 11th DAY OF OCTOBER 1975 THE SOCIETY OF PROFESSIONAL JOURNALISTS SIGMA DELTA CHI

ΣΔΧ

An award from Sigma Delta Chi, the Society of Professional Journalists.

Amid Civil War reenactments, CNN correspondent Peter Arnett gave the keynote address.

Amid considerable controversy over whether GATH meant the Arch to commemorate future correspondents and whether GATH's intrusion onto the Crampton's Gap battlefield should be perpetuated, a plaque was dedicated in October 2003 for journalists who were killed while covering the War on Terror in Iraq and Afghanistan. The plaque was the work of U.S. Army secretary Jack Marsh and Maryland Forest and Park Service superintendent Colonel Rich Barton, with the help of Maryland delegate Pete Callas of Washington County. It is dedicated to Daniel Pearl of the *Wall Street Journal*, Elizabeth Neuffer of the *Boston Globe*, David Bloom of NBC News and *Washington Post* columnist Michael Kelly.

The South Mountain State Battlefield was officially designated as Maryland's first state battlefield in 2001. At that time, then–park superintendent Dan Spedden wrote a grant that resulted in capital improvement funding for new museum interiors that were completed in 2013.

In Memory of Those Journalists Who Gave Their Lives
Reporting on the War on Terrorism

Daniel Pearl

The Wall Street Journal
Afghanistan - February 2002

David Bloom

NBC News
Iraq - April 2003

Michael Kelly

The Atlantic Monthly
The Washington Post
Iraq - April 2003

Elizabeth Neuffer

The Boston Globe
Iraq - April 2003

A marker at Gathland State Park dedicated to journalists who were killed in Iraq and Afghanistan in the War on Terror.

A ribbon cutting was held on May 11, 2013, at the Gathland and Washington Monument museums to introduce the public to the improved interpretive displays at the site. Along with the Gathland museum in the former Gapland Hall, a new museum was created in the Lodge, with displays depicting the Civil War battle fought at Crampton's Gap in 1862, just three days before the Battle of Antietam.

The nearby Washington Monument also received new displays that document how the monument was built by local Boonsboro residents in 1827, later repaired by a local civic organization and rehabilitated in the 1930s by the Civilian Conservation Corp. It also documents troop movements during the Civil War at that site.

A fifth generation of Townsend descendants, great-great-grandsons David Rasmussen and George Alfred Townsend IV, attended the ribbon cutting, and Mr. Townsend brought his children, the sixth generation of Townsends. David Rasmussen represented his mother, Dorothy Rasmussen, who was unable to make the trip but provided personal correspondence and photographs for this book and the University of Delaware archival collection.

Living history programs are presented at the Arch. Civil War reenactors stage encampments with authentic clothing and equipment and demonstrate

Civil War reenactors perform at the Arch.

the loading and firing of the park's cannon, a Napoleon twelve-pounder replica bought by the park for reenactments.

Few of GATH's splendid buildings remain, but the site is as beautiful, peaceful and bucolic as when GATH first discovered it. The State of

Maryland has nurtured the site with thoughtful planning, retaining its rustic charm while making it available to Civil War enthusiasts, Appalachian Trail hikers and visitors from Maryland, Pennsylvania, Virginia, West Virginia, Washington, D.C., and even farther afield. The park has become a splendid resource for everyone to enjoy history as well as natural beauty.

Appendix A

GENEALOGY CHART

Townsend Family Tree
(updated May 2014)

Rev. Stephen Townsend	m	Mary Milbourne
b. December 4. 1808		b. 1802
d. July 29, 1881		d. May 26, 1868

Julia Ann Wesley	George Edwin	Stephen Emory	George Alfred	Ralph Milbourne, MD
d. infancy	d. infancy	b. Dec. 3, 1835	b. Jan. 30, 1841	b. Feb. 21, 1845
		d. Apr. 19, 1856	d. Apr. 15, 1914	d. Dec. 11, 1877
			m. Bessie E. Rhodes	m. Ida Hollingsworth
			b. Mar. 20, 1842	
			d. May 30, 1903	

Genevieve Madeleine m. **Edmund F. Bonaventure**   Donn Piatt   Ella   **George Alfred , Jr.** m. Ila Rogers
b. Oct. 1866, Paris   *b. June 28, 1844   b. Dec. 23, 1871   b. Dec. 1, 1872   b. Jan 21, 1874
d. Dec. 8,1942   d. 1918   d. Mar. 9, 1875   d. Mar. 17, 1873   d. Feb. 5, 1948

Roger Gath m. Anne Mead (Oct. 1932)
b. August 19, 1907
d. Nov. 30, 1995

George Alfred	**Bessie**	**Genevieve**	**Yvonne**	**Simone**	**George Alfred III**	**Roger Gath, Jr.**
b. Jan. 2, 1885	b. 1886	b. 1887	b. 1891	b. 1906	b. Nov.14, 1943	b. Jul. 4, 1939
(went by Alfred)	d. 1886	d. 1970s	d. 1970	d. 54/55?	m. Jacqueline Engard	d. Jan. 4, 2011
m. Jeanne Elizabeth deKruijff						
b. 1890		m. Foster Ware	m. Nelson Goodwin	m. Jack Dyer		
d. 1971		9/30/1916				

Dorothy Elizabeth   **Genevieve**   **Cordelia**   **George Alfred Townsend IV**   **Roger Gath Townsend III, b. 1964**
b. June 17, 1923   d. age 7   b. 1924   b. Dec. 24, 1971   **Richard Mead Townsend, b. 1965**
m. William Rasmussen   d. 1969   m. Amy Elizabeth Hepburn,
b. Oct. 31, 1906   m. George Hall
d. Jan. 11, 1962

		Riley Hepburn, b. July 30, 2000
David Charles	**Elizabeth Jeanne**	Alec McKenzie, b. Sep. 14, 2002
b. May 9, 1949	b. Jan 22, 1954	Elizabeth Grace, b. July 7, 2006
	m. Douglas Forster	Anna Emeline, b. Jan. 7, 2009

Cassandra Kristine   b. Aug. 21, 1992

Sarah Kimberly Townsend
b. October 16, 1979
m. Jeremy Brandt Huvard, October 16, 2009

George Alfred III m. Nancy Lins   m. Sarita 1993/94
Michael b. 1986

*census records say 1846
*Listing of Bonaventure earlier family on page 126

Edmund F. Bonaventure Family

Edmund F. Bonaventure   b. 1844/1846   (earlier date is census figure)
m. Henriette Volkert   b. 1856
Edmund F   d. 1918/1920

Henriette Bonaventure   b. 1876   (married Flostroy)
Edmund Frances Charles   b. Apr. 22, 1873
Edmund Frances   b. 1878

m. Genevieve Townsend   May 28, 1884
b. Oct 6, 1866
d. December 8, 1942

George Alfred   b. 1885
Bessie   b. 1886/1886
Genevieve   b. 1887   m. Foster Ware   d. in 70's
                               Genevieve   d. age 7
                               Cordelia b. 1924, d. 1969 m. George Hall
Yvonne   b. 1891   m. Nelson Goodwin   d. in 70's
Simone   b. 1906   m. Jack Dyer   d. 54/55?

Appendix B

A Timeline of George Alfred Townsend and His Legacy through the Twentieth Century

1841	Born (Georgetown, DE)
1860	Graduated school (age nineteen)
1860	First job (*Philadelphia Inquirer*)
1861	Civil War (*New York Herald*)
1862–64	Europe sojourn
1864	Returned to United States and war
1865	Lincoln assassination (age twenty-four)
1865	Marriage to Bessie Rhodes
1866	Birth of daughter (Genevieve), in Paris
1867	Moved to Washington, D.C.
1874	Birth of son (Alfred)

1874	Moved to New York City
1884	Began building of Gapland
1881	Death of father Stephen Townsend
1888	Returned to Washington to live (divides time between D.C. and Gapland)
1896	Dedicated War Correspondents Arch
1903	Death of Bessie (Townsend is age sixty-two)
1914	Property deeded to Bonaventure
1914	Death of George Alfred Townsend (age seventy-three)
1918	Death of Bonaventure (property goes to daughter, Genevieve)
1922	Property sold to James Reid
1946	Fiftieth anniversary of the Arch
1958	Dedication of Gathland State Park
1996	Celebration of 100th anniversary
2013	Celebration of museum renovations

MAJOR WORKS
OF GEORGE ALFRED TOWNSEND

1861   *The Bohemians*, a play written when he was just twenty years old.

1865   *The Life, Crime and Capture of John Wilkes Booth*, a series of articles on Booth later bound as a book.

1866   *Campaigns of a Non-Combatant and His Romaunt Abroad*, articles about his experiences during the Civil War.

1867   *Life and Battles of Giuseppe Garibaldi and His March on Rome in* 1867, about the Italian liberator.

1867   *The Real Life of Abraham Lincoln*, an interview with Lincoln's law partner, William H. Herndon.

1869   *The New World Compared with the Old*, a serious book comparing European governments to those of the United Sates. It was his bestselling book.

1870   *Poems*, written after his marriage and return from Europe. Only three hundred copies printed.

1870 *Lost Abroad*, a book very similar to Twain's *Innocents Abroad*; not a major success.

1871 *Mormon Trials at Salt Lake City*, pamphlet that covered the Mormon Trials.

1873 *Washington, Outside and Inside*, an analysis of Washington's government.

1874 *New Washington, D.C.* (series of pamphlets) from the *Washington Chronicle*.

1876 *Events at the National Capitol and the Campaign of 1876*, summarizing government activities and scandals and political statistics; full biographies of Hayes, Wheeler, Tilden and Hendricks. Written with others.

1876 *Historical Sermons*, centennial sermons along the Mason-Dixon line, sketching old families.

1880 *Tales of the Chesapeake*, stories of people living on the Eastern Shore of Maryland, where Townsend spent part of his childhood.

1880 *Bohemian Days*, tales and poems of bygone days.

1881 *Poetical Addresses*, poems read at various ceremonies.

1884 *The Entailed Hat, or Patty Cannon's Times*, his most popular novel, regarding a notorious and very evil woman who trafficked in human flesh.

1885 *President Cromwell*, a drama in four acts.

1884 *Katy of Catoctin, or the Chain Breakers: A National Romance*, the novel he determined to write after covering Lincoln's assassination; it is a fictional accounting of Booth's supposed part in the plot to kill Lincoln. It was while researching this book that he found the land on which he built his summer estate twenty years later.

1890	*Mrs. Reynolds and Hamilton*, originally titled *Dr. Priestley, of the Federalists.*
1892	*Columbus in Love*, a pamphlet that originally appeared in *Lippincott's.*
1899	*Poems of Men and Events*, a shortened collection of older poems and new ones, with illustrations of his family and his mountaintop estate.
1902	*Monticello and Its Preservation Since Jefferson's Death*, recounts the story of Uriah Phillips Levy, who bought and restored Monticello.

Of the thousands and thousands of shorter articles that had been published in newspaper or magazines, some were grouped by subject and reprinted as pamphlets or small books, and sold separately. Others were published but have not survived. Some of his poems and parts of books were drastically reduced by the publisher, and many of his works were unpublished.

A LOCAL POET'S TRIBUTE TO GATH

*T*om Harbaugh was a novelist and poet in the Middletown Valley and immortalized GATH in a poem that appeared in the *Middletown Register* in October 1920, six years after his death. It was printed again on the fiftieth-anniversary celebration of the dedication of the War Memorial Arch in 1946.

GAPLAND

All's silent now where long ago
The merry jest passed to and fro;
Gone are the guests who once did come
To grace the long-dead master's home,
And share his board and drink his wines
Where softly creep the idle vines.

Today the spider spins her thrall,
And vacancy is over all;
With gentle slope the mountains rise
To peaks that seek the cloudless skies,
And overhead on silent wing
The lay buzzards slowly swing.

What feasts were here! What happy hours
Were passed among the scented flow'rs
What tales were told, what strains of song
Were sung, the moments to prolong!
No more, no more the feast is spread.
The master's gone; his guests are dead.

Ghosts seem to haunt the lonely place,
No more is seen the pleasing face,
The seasons come, the seasons go
With summer shine and winter snow,
And over Gapland far and near
Comes down anon a haunted fear.

Night seals with black the voiceless wood,
The hares come out in search of food,
No sound is heard, no laugh is there,
From lips go up no song nor pray'r;
The very air is damp and chill
As winds possess the weird hill

O Gapland fair, embowered deep,
May you awaken from your sleep,
And know once more that past that's fled—
The past that seems forever dead;
Then will your fame return and then
You'll be the home of living men;
But now over path and crumbling wall
There hangs a dark and silent pall.

BIBLIOGRAPHY

Association of American Geographers. *Middle Atlantic Division Field Report*. May 25, 1968

Brunswick (MD) Herald. "The Latest from the Last Century." 1893.

Frederick Daily News. "Notice of Deed of Transfer for property at Gapland to Edmund F. Bonaventure." April 27, 1914.

GATH. "GATH Talks About His Den." *Cincinnati Enquirer*, September 24, 1891.

GATH. "Harpers Ferry, a Restatement of the John Brown Raid, Existing Impressions, the Thrilling Story Rehearsed." *Chicago Tribune*, December, 1870.

GATH. "An Interviewer Interviewed." *Lippincott's Monthly Magazine*, November 1891.

GATH. "The Press." *New York Tribune*, June 28, 1879.

GATH. "Reflections and Recollections." *Lippincott's Monthly Magazine*, November 1886.

GATH. "Salt River." *New York Tribune*, March 4, 1881.

Haller, Harry. "Gapland's Crumbling Ruins." *Baltimore Sun*, December 16, 1936.

Hamilton, W.R. "A Famous Author's Home in the South Mountains." *Baltimore Sun*, August 25, 1907.

Hindes, Ruthanna. *George Alfred Townsend, One of Delaware's Outstanding Writers*. Dover: Delaware Heritage Press, 1946.

Hudson, William C. "A Figure in Journalism." *Brooklyn Eagle*, April 1914.

Lagemann, Roger. "Historic Structures Report, Part I: War Correspondents Arch." National Park Service, May 18, 1961.

Murphy, John. "George Alfred Townsend, 19th Century Cosmopolite." *Maryland Magazine* 14, no. 2 (1980).

Noyes, Crosby S. "The Unique Monument at Gapland." *Washington Evening Star*, October 16, 1896.

Perry, James M. *A Bohemian Brigade: The Civil War Correspondents—Mostly Rough, Sometimes Ready*. New York: Wiley and Sons, 2000.

Reese, Timothy. "Fair Cause, Unfair Placement." *Hagerstown (MD) Herald Mail*, October 19, 2003.

Savoyard. "Dean of the Cloth: George Alfred Townsend Heads Washington Correspondents." *Washington Evening Star*, February 26, 1911.

Shields, Jerry. *Gath's Work and Literary Folk*. Dover: Delaware Heritage Press, 1996.

Snyder, Betty M. "Maryland Author's Home in Ruins." *Baltimore Sun*, December 13, 1925.

Townsend, George Alfred. *Campaigns of a Non-Combatant*. New York: Blelock, 1886.

Valley Register (Middletown, MD). "The Gapland Road Trouble." October 18, 2012.

Other Resources

Archives of A. Aubrey Bodine

Archives at Gathland State Park, much of which were obtained from archives at the Maryland Department of Natural Resources

Friends of Gathland, later Friends of South Mountain Battlefield

Letters of George Alfred Townsend, private collection of Dorothy Rasmussen

Maryland Hall of Records

University of Delaware

INDEX

ABOUT THE AUTHOR

*D*ianne Wiebe has had several careers since launching herself into the work world. After creating and providing an innovative program for handicapped adults, she moved to directing nonprofits. In a fortunate convergence, she found herself able to combine architectural preservation and main street revitalization efforts to create a fusion of progress and protection at a statewide level.

For ten years in upstate New York, she was a journalist, writing news and feature articles for the *Kingston Daily Freeman*, the *Shawangunk Journal* and several other local papers. She also worked as communications and publications director for the Redemptorist Fathers at Mount St. Alphonsus Retreat Center, and for the Ellenville School District. Ms. Wiebe successfully combined skills in writing, photography and layout and design to produce high-quality publications and several books. She is co-author and publisher of a nonfiction book titled *Yama Farms, a Most Unusual Resort*, set in rural New York.